Free Range Blessings

A Journey from Family Farm
to Successful Business with Eggs and Faith

Margaret Farrelly

10-10-10
Publishing

Publisher
10-10-10 Publishing
Markham, ON
Canada

Printed in Canada and the United States of America

Dedication

My thanks to Killian, our son, whose idea it was to write a book in the first place. To Leo who provided the financial support and patiently waited for results, and to family members and others who helped with shaping the chapters and the pages. To Anne Marie and Jimmy for allowing me to get to know so much about their darling daughter Aoibheann.

Testimonials

One of the joys of working in the restaurant industry and making my TV programs is that I meet many of our wonderful food producers. Margaret Farrelly is one such person, and we have always used her eggs in Mac Nean House & Restaurant. The quality is second to none. Usually, we don't get to know the story behind the business, so I was fascinated to read Margaret's account of how Clonarn Clover got to where it is today, from a small beginning over twenty years ago. The book is full of good advice that gives me pause for thought. Congratulations Margaret.

—**Neven Maguire**
Celebrity Chef, Author & Restauranteur

When I'm in Margaret's presence I feel safe. There is a very positive and spiritual presence around her. There is a naturalness and modesty about all that she does, and we can all learn from Margaret's journey. This book could be a manual for a business model or a guide to how to be the perfect Irish lady, but in truth it's both of these things, and much more. A must read; you will instantly feel better about yourself after reading this book.

Margaret is one of Ireland's leading food champions and one of life's ladies, and I'm the better for having met and known her.

—**Brian Mc Dermott**
Celebrity Chef, Author & Restauranteur

Having grown up in rural Cavan, I can identify with the wonderful insights in Margaret Farrelly's book, *Free Range Blessings*. This is a gem of a book that captures the soul of what it takes to create a successful family business. What stands out is Margaret and her husband Leo's great faith, and how it became interwoven into every aspect of their lives, helping them bounce back from many challenges. Their commitment to each other and to their family is inspiring, as is their commitment to being the very best in the world at what they do. This book contains so many business insights about the importance of passion, quality, innovation, customer service and plain hard work. Above all else it is packed with key life lessons effortlessly woven into an inspirational and uplifting book about respect for others, gratitude for the many blessings they have received and, above all else, about love. Everyone should read this book.

—Sean Gallagher
**Entrepreneur, former investor on Dragon's Den TV show and bestselling author of *Secrets to Success- Inspiring Stories from Leading Entrepreneurs*
www.seangallagher.com**

I well remember the first time I came across Margaret Farrelly. She'd been nominated for the FBD/IFJ Women & Agriculture Awards, and as I read her application the more in awe I became of this unassuming lady.

Like Margaret and many farming women, I got into a few hens in the 1980s, but between the fox and everything else I ended up with no hens. At the same time, Margaret turned her 150 hens into a multimillion-euro enterprise directly employing over 35 people as well as supporting 20 neighbouring farmers who supply free range eggs to her business.

Her account of how this was achieved makes *Free Range Blessings* an essential read for anyone with a family business, or thinking about setting one up.

Margaret doesn't sugar-coat how tough the early years were for her husband Leo and herself and their young family, when everything was driven by necessity. It wasn't easy making a living on 33 acres, and the hens had to deliver.

But it was the early 1980's when people were prepared to spend more of their disposable income on what they perceived to be a higher quality product. And that's what Margaret aimed to deliver. She would never compete on price. Her focus was on supplying the very best product on the market. And so Clonarn Clover Ltd was born.

To do all this you need happy and contented hens, and it would be no exaggeration to say that Margaret loves and respects her hens. These are hens that get cuddles, and when considering their needs Margaret tries to put herself in their place: *What would my hens want or like?* She is in awe of their ability to make an egg every day, and after reading her book so am I.

While the scale of the business grew from packing 1,800 eggs an hour to 36,000 an hour, Margaret also looked to innovation to grow the business. Omega 3 enrichment, white shelled eggs, dealing with large and small eggs, pasteurisation and DNA recognition are all part of the innovation process.

Margaret's deep faith in God is the golden thread that weaves its way all through this book. Her love of Medugorje as a place of pilgrimage sings from the pages. Her deep faith helped her cope with not just the deaths of her parents and young sister Mary, but also with the challenges brought on by the business.

That faith was challenged at a time of great need when Leo, her darling husband, was seriously injured in a car accident. With intense honesty she admits asking God not to leave Leo with the family if he was going to require full-time care. She says she didn't have what it took to mind someone whose every need was her responsibility. Thankfully Leo made a full recovery.

There are many happy stories in this book, and I dare you not to laugh at the antics of 'Tweeny' and 'Miss Cheeky.' There's the powerful account of the work of 'Aoibheann's Pink Tie' and other charities Margaret has been drawn to support.

Margaret went on to win the Women & Agriculture Awards. She

then represented Ireland in the European awards and so impressed the judges that she beat off entrants from the 27 EU member states to win the European On Farm Innovation award.

Was I surprised? Not a bit. Margaret Farrelly is a special lady who gives so much and whose every action comes from sheer goodness and a deep faith in God. Her book is a ray of positivity in these uncertain times.

—Mairead Lavery is a former editor of *Irish Country Living*, a popular weekly family supplement of the *Irish Farmers Journal*. As editor she worked with a team to introduce the Women & Agriculture Awards and the annual Women & Agriculture conference. Prior to this she worked as a journalist with the paper.

Table of Contents

Acknowledgements

Thinking back to those early days when my parents helped us get set up initially, I recall with gratitude the empowering visits from two wonderful women who were our poultry advisers. Not only did they encourage us to follow our intuition but they in no small way prepared us for a future that perhaps they alone could foresee. Thanks to the men and women who became poultry farmers and trusted us to find a market for their eggs. I recall those evenings when the business was still only part time. Each producer arrived in turn and stayed to help grade their eggs turning our modest egg store into somewhat of a social center where great friendships were formed.

In those early days the support of the Cavan County Development office, now Cavan LEO (Local Enterprise Office), was very much appreciated and helped us acquire equipment, broaden our knowledge, and offered opportunities to learn more about our industry and changing markets through "Best Practice" visits abroad.

The need for permanent staffing came with the decision turn the eggs into a full-time venture. Each and every staff member who crossed our paths since then has played their own part in shaping my story. Another group of people without whom the story of Margaret's would not have happened are our loyal customers, who stuck with us through thick and thin. Of course, we would have a very small business if it were not for all the wonderful shoppers who week after week put a pack of Margaret's eggs in their shopping basket.

Family members and friends mentioned within the pages of this book contributed in no small way either as they were, and continue to be, fundamental in developing the person that I am. To you I owe the deepest debt of gratitude.

Please forgive me if I single out two girls for a special mention. These young girls lost their battle with cancer over a quarter of a century apart and in a way appear to have connected to complete one cycle of my life. My late sister Mary, who died in 1982, and little Aoibheann Norman, who I did not know in this life, lost her battle in 2010 at only 8 years of age. I believe these two beautiful girls lovingly pulled at my strings and nudged me into taking the final step in putting pen to paper.

I remain deeply indebted to each one mentioned above.

Foreword

Free Range Blessings: A Journey from Family Farm to Successful Business with Eggs and Faith is the journey of one Irish woman into the world of free-range egg production and how her faith impacted many of the choices that led her family's business to success. Along the way, she gives you an entertaining and insightful look into how eggs are produced, packed, and make their way to your local grocery shelves.

Margaret's story also captures a slice of Irish life during the late 20th century. Her personal history is full of moments where her faith clearly served as a guide, from her choice of husband to dealing with the grief of losses within her family. She also shares cultural changes in Ireland as well, introducing you to life in rural Ireland.

Free Range Blessings is an inspiring story that touches on the lives of a family building a unique business and how their focus on faith and family has guided the growth of their livelihood. Along the way, you will also get introduced to the amazing egg and what it means to be a free-range egg producer.

If you are starting a business or at a crossroads with your current one, then *Free Range Blessings: A Journey from Family Farm to Successful Business with Eggs and Faith* is an inspiring book that can help you see what is possible when you are willing to take a leap of faith and work hard to achieve your goals.

Raymond Aaron
New York Times Bestselling Author

CHAPTER ONE

The Growth of
The Farrelly Family Tree

"I have a bit of a confession to make. We weren't actually making Helping Hands." With that, the words were taken out of my mouth. "I'm a farmer from Cavan. We have a reasonably successful farm-based business at home, and I want to share some of our good fortune with you."

There I stood, in a Charity Kitchen in the Liberties, with two women that I only met a week ago and had developed an admiration for that no words can describe. Their eyes brimmed with tears, trying to accept what the revelation meant for them. I myself, having lived among this inner-city Dublin community for the past week, was reeling with emotions as I revealed my real purpose to them. The words "Secret Millionaire" did not fit well on my shoulders but that was the name of the program and I was simply sharing some of our good fortune and success with people I considered less well off than us.

It was a week that I will never forget. Sometimes even now I can't help wondering "How in goodness name did we get here?" Yet I cannot help feeling that our experience could perhaps encourage others particularly in the unprecedented difficult landscape that is 2020. With that in mind I hope to show in the coming pages how it is possible for ordinary people to achieve success in life and how our humble simple background, our unrelenting needs as young parents, our determination, trust and most of all our naivety contributed to what is our story. Faith too played a huge part and how believing that everything happens for a reason helped in overcoming numerous hardships.

The Family Roots

My own story began on July 12th, 1952, when I presented as the first of 4 children to James and Anna Fegan. James and Anna were modest and unassuming people, epitomizing the people of their day. Daddy was the breadwinner, a blacksmith by trade, primarily shoeing horses, fixing cartwheels, and repairing and maintaining farm machinery. It is difficult to imagine in the modern Ireland of today how life was in the 50's and 60's. Almost all work in the country was manual and very labor intensive. Those who were lucky had a horse and whatever machinery necessary to enable them to get the crops sown and harvested, to draw the milk to the creamery and owning a horse drawn trap which provided the family with transport was considered a luxury.

James and Anna Fegan's wedding (November 1949)

Unfortunately, or maybe fortunately the demands of the modernizing world meant farming in Ireland had to shift from the traditional and quite literal workhorse to the tractor. Within a few years, blacksmith work had diminished but daddy who was a young healthy resourceful man reinvented himself, adapting his trade to become what would probably be called an engineer in today's world.

Along with being hard working, mammy too was a resourceful person. Like so many other women, she was the home maker, looking after the house and family and maintaining a garden where she grew vegetables and kept a few poultry for eggs and meat. Mammy worked hard and was always thinking of ways to bring in a few extra shillings. She raised a few pigs and milked four cows, supplying the milk to our local creamery and sometimes making her own butter. She was also very creative and skilled with her hands, making saleable items like bedside lamps and tweed pictures, while frequently remodeling clothes for us.

Tweed picture

In an era when Ireland was becoming electrified the lamps were and ideal gift and the collage type pictures which were made using pieces of Irish Tweed fabric to depict countryside scenes were a real hit with visiting emigrants especially with Irish-American visitors. In this sense, Mammy was an innovator, and while very small, was typical of the women that spawned the era of the cottage industries. Although our lives were simple, we had everything we needed, and every day and every mealtime was packed full with love.

Margaret helping with feeding piglets 1954

Margaret's First Communion 1959

Sean's First Holy Communion Jimmy & Margaret's confirmation 1964

The 4 Fegan children 1968

In May 1955, I got my first little brother Jimmy, followed 2 years later by Sean. February 13ᵗʰ, 1964, the three of us arrived home from school to dinner "by daddy." As daddy's cooking was so rare, I can still remember that meal, a pot of boiled potatoes with eggs mashed into them which we all agreed tasted just gorgeous even though we were a little scared, wondering, "Where was mammy?" Once we had eaten, Daddy sent us to our bedroom. Some hours later he came in the room to tell us we had a new baby sister. Such innocence, not even myself who was almost 12 years old suspected that mammy was having a baby. Later at about 8 pm, we were introduced to our sister Mary. We were all besotted with her and Jimmy who formed an instant bond with her declared "Is she real, Is she really ours"? Our parents and grandparents often spoke of the War and the Emergency but for us life seemed quite normal. However, those previous years instilled a culture of "Waste not, want not," into a generation of people teaching them to be thrifty and foster a culture of generosity. While I am sure that my parents struggled at times to provide, it was clear that providing for the family was their priority and working hard was just the "way of life." Not even once do I remember either parent complain but I do recall finding Mammy crying silently on a few occasions and on one occasion I remember daddy unexplainably finding it hard to get out of bed and face the day. Mammy worked her magic with a concoction of Buckfast Tonic Wine and raw eggs and daddy was back on his feet in no time at all with a renewed bubbling spirit!

They placed a huge priority on education. Visualizing an easier life for us they believed that by working hard they could provide us with opportunities that they themselves did not have. We were privileged, as many of our generation didn't finish their schooling. In fact, many people from that era struggle with reading and writing even today. Emphasis was also placed on taking responsibility for certain duties. Looking back, it is clear that we were given responsibility for a reason. For the most part, our responsibilities included helping mammy in the house, but also by walking the cows to their paddocks as we walked to school. Then as we made the return journey, we would bring the cows back home with us. As we entered our teenage years, we found part-time work. Ironically enough, my first job was occasionally gathering eggs on a neighbour's poultry farm.

Later, I found weekend and summer work in The Park Hotel in Virginia. Owned by the McDonald family, it was very prestigious, and the standards were high. Here I learned the importance of attention to detail. We were expected to get the job done promptly and right first time which propelled the development of a pride in my work that has stood me in good stead throughout my life, to this very day.

My first permanent job was in the clearing department of one of Irelands main banks, which meant a move to Dublin. It was a new way of life, with the constant hustle and bustle. I worked hard in the clearing department, before moving up the professional ladder. In fact, I became Assistant Manager at the age of 27. It was unprecedented at that time for a woman of my age to be given a position of such responsibility, but we were just coming to the end of the age of chivalry.

Out on My Own

Born in 1952, I entered a fast-changing world. The benefit of a second level education was just becoming a realization in Ireland. While my parents were indeed qualified in their own right, they did not experience the luxury of a lengthy formal education. They did, however, recognise that times were changing and so adapted. It was years later when my siblings and I grasped how challenging this must have been for them. Having attended a small country school, once referred to by my aunt as "Lattoon University", I transferred to Ballyjamesduff convent school for my last two years of primary education. Here, in the all-girls' school, the nuns prepared us for "life". I was a smart enough kid, and along with being a little bit lazy, was incredibly shy. I know now that lack of confidence restricted me, but back then I directed my preference to "blending in". There were occasions though where I overcame that inhibition, driven by a will to make something happen. I guess I believed in Henry Ford's philosophy, "Whether you believe you can, or you can't, you are right." With the right will, all things are possible! I remember "learning to drive." That was some challenge! I made up my mind to buy a car, and so driving would then become the natural next step. I'd had many failed attempts, but once I made my mind up, the job was as good as done! On the second weekend after getting my car and without any experience of city driving, I drove back to Dublin, much to the horror of my brother Sean. Once I took the notion to do something, wild horses could not stop me.

Parents generally want to give their children a better life perhaps than they had themselves, pushing them further up the ladder and we had that type of parent. Baby Boomers worked to break glass ceilings and make college a reality for their children. Generation X parents have children who work the gadgets better than they do. Every generation is trying to reach a little higher and explore or achieve more than the one before. Both our parents belonged to the Greatest Generation, whose lasting characteristic was a strong work ethic. The sense of entitlement we experience today was nonexistent.

After secondary school, I took a secretarial course, which I completed in 1971. Ireland was very different in the early 1970s versus today. In those days, many girls followed a career in nursing or teaching, both of which required further education. The rest found jobs in the Civil Service, Post Office, Aer Lingus or the banks. Being the oldest in our house, it was just normal that I go working after secondary school and so I was encouraged to apply for those good pensionable jobs, as mammy called them. My application to the Bank was a bit of a disaster. Behind mammy's back, I completed the application in red ink and turned it in late and without the necessary passport style photo of myself. I really didn't want to work in the bank, because the job specification stated a high level of shorthand and typing. I was hopeless at these, but despite my attempt at sabotage, I was called for an interview and hired. I never actually needed that awful shorthand in the job, so "happy days." My commitment to myself showed through in my work. I became assistant manager after only 8 years of service, being one of the youngest girls to receive such a position and was doing alright for myself. Nevertheless, I was still that shy quiet girl from County Cavan, who was happy to stand out without sticking out.

In 1972, the Irish government removed the ban on girls working after marriage. I know it is hard to imagine nowadays but girls were encouraged to work in those good pensionable jobs, as retirement on marriage was somewhat compensated by the "marriage gratuity", which was calculated according to the years of service given prior to leaving. I had my good pensionable job where I formed new friendships with people from all over Ireland, and some of those friendships still exist right to this very day. My two brothers, when their turns came, were afforded the opportunity to train as woodwork teachers. I did not feel jealous of this as I somehow remember getting great satisfaction from being able to help at home. From the age of sixteen, I took great delight in giving my pay packet to mammy each week. I had no need for money, as in those days we did not go out socialising until about the age of 18 years old or older.

My job in the Bank saw me take up a position in Donnybrook, Dublin. While I was definitely a shy country girl, deep down I had a sense of fun, which came out in my love of dancing. Living in Dublin and accessibility to several venues facilitated dancing every night of the week, so I danced every night except Saturday. As Sunday mornings were still reserved for one's weekly religious duty, Saturday nights were considered kind of sacred and reserved for early to bed.

A Sunday night dance in the country meant an early hitch-hike back to Dublin for work at 9 am. Each day I was at work at 8:45 am, regardless of how late I had stayed out the night before. Sometimes I would go to bed after work to "recharge the batteries" for another night's dancing with friends. During the 1970s, country music from America was big and I loved it. It simply carried me away. Even sad songs, by such artists as Tammy Wynette, Loretta Lynn, Dolly Parton, Jim Reeves or Porter Waggoner, would lift my spirits. There was just something about that music that touched my soul and made my feet tap. Even today, 50 years later the music has that same effect on my soul and my feet! Sadly, the dancing fell victim of my changing lifestyle many years ago but the satisfaction of engaging in time consuming new ventures more than compensated.

After 12 years in Dublin, in 1982 I went to a dance in Cootehill and there I met Leo. He wanted to buy me a drink. I asked for water because I didn't have much interest in alcohol. Keep in mind, the bottled water craze was not yet popular in Ireland. Water came from a tap and was free, so Leo wasn't willing to ask for that from the bar. It just wouldn't have been very gentlemanly in his mind. I ended up having to get my own drink that first night. The drink aside, that was a fun and memorable Easter Sunday night. In fact, we still joke about this every now and again, but in the intervening years, he has bought me practically anything I wanted.

Mammy described that night as "the night Margaret struck oil." She liked Leo very much and it was her way of showing approval.

When he asked me out, I couldn't say no. His kindness and warmth were so visible to me and the gentleness and sincerity he oozed was only surpassed in my mind by the image of his beautiful brown eyes. The mutual attraction grew and grew and within a very short time I realized how important faith was in his life and that warmed my heart also. Faith was a foundation of my life and it was important that my partner in life have that same foundation. Dancing, talking and joking with each other led us to a lifelong, loving relationship.

Leo was a 1952 baby also and the youngest of the four Farrelly children. He had grown up about 10 miles away from my home place and at the time we met he tended to his family's farm. There was something special about him. As the months passed, Leo and I were dating, and everything seemed to be going from strength to strength. Our relationship truly proved to be a brightness during what was to be a difficult and sad time for the Fegan family.

A Tragic Loss

In 1980, my treasured little sister Mary was feeling tired and listless, particularly in the mornings. She was 12 years younger than me and it seemed as if she was a bundle of energy that could just keep going forever, especially at night. At first, Mammy blamed the late nights with friends and the long journey to London during the Easter holiday with her school, for the tiredness.

On my birthday, I returned home from Dublin to spend time with the family, only to find that Mary was very unwell. Mammy said the normal doctor was on holiday and a different one said that it was just a virus. However, by the time I got home, her small and ring fingers on her left hand were numb and she had no feeling on the left side of her tongue. Mammy didn't want to call the doctor, because she believed he had been quite dismissive and would give her very little heed. I made the call and when the doctor heard about the numbness, he got a bit panicked and suggested we bring Mary to Cavan General Hospital for x-rays. At the hospital, we were told it was her nerves and she was prescribed medication.

Mary was adamant that it was not her imagination. We went back to the doctor, who overreacted to Mammy's persistence. "Jaysus Christ,

Mam, there wouldn't be a thing wrong with the child if you would stop fussing over her!"

Our family is a determined lot. My sister-in-law worked as a theatre nurse in a local hospital. She talked with an orthopedic surgeon there who agreed to see Mary. He referred her to an eye specialist on the following Monday, who instantly saw the pressure of the glioma on the optic nerve and referred her to St. Vincent's Hospital in Dublin. There she was assigned to a capable young neurosurgeon, Christopher Pidgeon, who had just returned from America. In August 1980, our beautiful 16-year-old sister had a tumor the size of a golf ball removed from her brain. I was fortunate to be working close to St. Vincent's, so I was able to visit every day. One evening, a few days after her surgery I brought her bananas as they were a favorite. Mary did not recognise the banana, yet she was able to make comments about other patients through the Irish language. What an amazing and complicated organ the brain is!

Mary before her illness

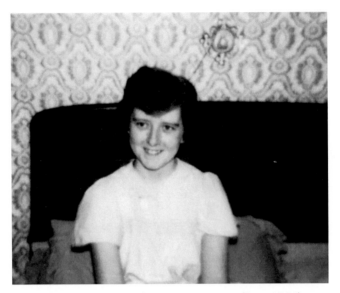

Mary 14 mths into her cancer journey (Sept 1981)

Cancer in young people at that time was very rare and treatment was underdeveloped. She returned to school in October of that year, but then suffered an aggressive epileptic fit that required her to be hospitalized. She didn't return to school again. With the only form of treatment at the time being radiation, which was administered as a last resort, Mary struggled along. In December 1981, she was admitted to St. Vincent's and then transferred to St. Luke's in Dublin for radiation treatment. Early 1982 was difficult, as the radiation did its work. There was no anti-nausea medicine then, but we heard no complaints from Mary.

On St. Stephen's Day in 1981 in St Vincent's hospital, Mary greeted mammy & I saying, "I decided something today. If you all don't mind, I'm happy to die." Hearing that from a 17-year-old is not easy, and she only shared these thoughts with one other person, her dear friend Cynthia. In June of 1982 as Mary's sight, speech and other faculties were fading, Mammy told her that I had a new boyfriend that she, mammy thought he might be here to stay. Mary's response was simply to lift her hand and whisper, "That's good." Those were the last time she spoke. She died on September 24, 1982.

This period was a roller coaster ride of emotions for me. On one hand, but very gently my relationship with Leo was developing into something very special. I had the butterflies in my stomach, can't eat and can't sleep, generated excitement and a realisation of those true love feelings. I experienced feelings of guilt at being happy when really the saddest event was also developing. Jimmy too experienced similar feelings as he and his wife had their first baby in March which should have been a time for the whole family to celebrate. Sean on the other hand had just started dating a girl from Mary's school. So many emotions!!!! Well of course everyone was very happy, but Mary's deteriorating condition was a constant dark shadow on our lives. The thought of losing Mary was unthinkable.

Our faith was an anchor during this dark time, although focusing on praying was extremely difficult and indeed at times praying seemed a waste of time. We prayed for the strength to accept God's Holy Will for Mary. During her illness, Mary's own faith was so evident. She made two pilgrimages to Our Lady's Shrine at Lourdes with our diocese, despite the continuing loss of her facilities as part of her illness. Her trust in God made her happy to leave the suffering of this world and move on to the next.

We did not realise it at the time but her acceptance of how sick she was and her acceptance of her impending death, particularly at such a young age had a profound effect on us all. The family had a strong faith, but can I say at this point that our faith was well tested. While there were times that anger and doubt prevailed and it was really hard not to resent our loss, ultimately, we drew on the Mary's example and used our faith to help us with accepting the inevitable.

Here's where Leo showed his true nature and respect for others, characteristics which highlighted his warm personality, triggering the breathtaking realization that we loved one another. He was so supportive and strong towards the end of Mary's illness and after her death, not only for me but my entire family. His empathy came from firsthand knowledge. He too had dealt with the tragedy of cancer as a young boy. His mother, Annie, had been diagnosed with breast cancer while Leo was young, and she spent the last 7 years of her life in and out of hospitals. His memories are of a loving mother who never complained. In early 1965, she entered the hospital for the last time. The hospital was in Dublin, making it difficult for the family to visit her, but they made sure to visit on Sundays. A few hours after returning home from visiting on Sunday December 8th that year, they received the awful news that Annie had passed. There was no grief counseling then, only the harsh attitude that you "get on with it". Annie's influence shines through in Leo, even though he only had a few precious years with her. Leo had a great love for my mother & father and I believe this was because of losing his own mother when he was only 12 years old.

Farrelly family Michael, Granny Farrelly, Annie & Tommy (Leo's parents)
& Alice. Front row Leo & Anne

A man of such respect, Leo allowed my family time and space to grieve and on the 8th of March 1983 his own birthday, he proposed. I immediately said, "YES!" We got married just a few months later in July 1983, opening a new chapter of our lives, a new beginning full of hope. Strange as it might seem our marriage and my return to living near my parents helped them greatly also. By our second anniversary, we were about to become parents ourselves, to the first of our four children.

Our Wedding July 1983

As we welcomed our beautiful black-haired, brown-eyed little girl, it didn't take us long to pick a name, Annemarie, in honor of Leo's mother Annie and my sister Mary. Life was beginning to look brighter again with mammy spenting a lot of time with us and the new baby. It wasn't long before baby number 2 was on the way, and to our delight, in January 1987 our beautiful Aileen arrived. With our little family growing in size, Leo being the breadwinner began to realise that the small family farm would not be able to support us into the future and was looking for ways to diversify. By chance, as he read through the local paper one weekend, he saw an advertisement looking for small farmer enterprises to get into free-range egg production. We decided to make enquires. After getting a few answers, the decision was made to get some hens. Looking back, I can't remember this being a particularly difficult decision. Perhaps it is the benefit of hindsight has given me rose-tinted glasses, but I think it just felt right for us. We made a deal with the packer and started our life as egg farmers. I fell completely in love with the hens as soon as they arrived and quickly found that when you are doing something you love; it really isn't work at all. In fact, I exaggerate as I was in love with the creatures before the new additions arrived but I just had more of them to love!

Our first venture was a tiny flock of 150 hens. It didn't take long till we saw the benefits the little hens brought. Not only were they their own little enterprise on the farm, we always had fresh eggs for ourselves. Not to mention, how they stole my heart as I cared for and bonded with them. The 33-acre farm had been home to mixed farming for generations, all-in-all there had been beef cattle, dairy cattle, tillage, and potatoes. When Leo took over the farm, he had focused on growing the dairy herd, which was still a strong feature in the early years that we had hens.

Leo and I made a great team, working to our strengths. Things weren't always automated as they are now. A prime example of this was that feed had to be carried into the hen house and put into tube feeders to allow the hens to eat to their desire throughout the day. While Leo took care of the more labour-intensive aspects, like carrying in the feed, I would pick the eggs and manage the birds, allowing Leo to look after the other animals on the farm. Leo was hopeless at the paperwork, so my training from the bank and dare I admit that awful secretarial course, came in handy for managing the records for the farm overall.

Within a year we started grading and packing our own eggs, growing our production flock numbers to meet with customers' demand. The hen and her marvelous egg were about to change our lives even more. I was in the middle of another love affair, this time with these amazing little creatures that I believe are taken far too much for granted and are grossly under rated in the food chain.

Leo, AnneMarie & Margaret grading eggs in 1997

CHAPTER TWO

The Marvel of the Egg

With all that has happened in the last 40 years the recession of the 1980's is almost a distant memory at this stage. However, I am reminded frequently that "timing is everything" and our entry into the world of commerce when we did was no coincidence. We were not aware of the significance at the time, but we were entering an era when people were willing to spend more of their disposable income on what they perceived to be a higher quality product. Relatively quickly, Leo and I realized that the market was growing more than our girls could cater for and so we decided to buy eggs from local farms who like ourselves saw an opportunity to have some extra farm income and applied to become free range egg suppliers to our business. It was an exciting time for our family, as our little company was growing. Leo kept farming in the more traditional sense, maintaining his small dairy herd and a small flock of sheep, through continued slow but steady growth in the egg business; Nearly unbeknownst to us the hens and eggs were starting to demand more time. Leo nearly exclusively done the deliveries, while I ran the day-to-day aspects of the business, managing the eggs, the grading, planning future production and looking after the kids.

The first 10 years of business, well, it would be a lie to say it was easy, but the business itself was not overly distressing. Those days definitely gave more joy than grief and still trigger such pleasant thoughts on reflection. Perhaps this was due to the rate of growth, perhaps it was the personalities of Leo & I always quickly seeking solutions to problems and pushing forward, perhaps it was the characteristics that we could see in the little hens that we became so passionate about; or maybe even the genuine people who crossed our paths whether they became customers or suppliers, but these years gave us and the business an unyielding foundation for the future. After creating a loyal customer base, taking the challenges as they came and turning them into a learning experience rather than becoming disheartened, our 10-year anniversary became a defining year for the company. We had already taken the practical decision for our family in the mid-90's to concentrate our future plans on the poultry and started reducing the sheep flock and dairy herd. This consequentially empowered us to grasp at an opportunity that came our way in 1998, when we bought a successful, homely, albeit small brand called "Brownstead Free Range Eggs", a highly recognized Free-Range brand in Dublin city. This acquisition increased our presence in the Dublin Market and led to a 35% inRTA 1996rease in our overall throughput. No longer were we just the small local brand "Farrelly's Eggs," but herein was the birth of Clonarn Clover Ltd. and a brand-new excitement and enthusiasm driving us. With growth came the realization that we would need to expand our facilities and this we did with the construction of a new facility in 2000 which was kitted out with brand new modern equipment in 2001. These were exciting times bringing with them extra staff, extra responsibilities, new customers and new business from existing customers.

Our strategic decision to concentrate our business on Free range exclusively, meant we were never ever going to be able to compete on price so our focus on supplying "The very BEST product on the market", became our corner stone! We were so busy keeping our heads down and getting on with life we had not realised that consumer attitudes were changing. How lovely to discover that Animal welfare was becoming more of a priority and the suitability of cages for laying hens was being called into question. The consumer's desire to buy ethically produced food was becoming a huge factor in deciding what food to put on the table and indeed which producer of the preferred choice was also becoming a greater factor when shopping. We were ahead of the curve as our hens were already like family but now the consumer wanted to hear about this and indeed learn more.

As the children grew up, their help with both the farm and the business was welcome. Time has shown us just how much those early days shaped our family's philosophy. We felt assured that the company ethos would continue into the future and it was a source of both joy and pride to see the children involving themselves in and taking on their own little roles within the family and business. The most satisfying thing of all was that the children maintained such respect for the hens. They were more animal oriented than commercially motivated, thus enabling us to stick with the more traditional farming ways rather than chasing after volume at lower prices, which might be considered a risk to animal welfare or product quality.

The egg produced in this traditional way was indeed recognizably a different egg and increasingly sought after.

The Miracle Egg

Eggs are laid by females in multiple species. While not all eggs get eaten, a few bird and reptile eggs make the cut, due to their hard eggshell, albumen (egg white) and vitellus (egg yolk). For centuries now, hen eggs are the most popular, and for more than 3 decades the hen egg has been hugely beneficial to our family providing us with a prosperous business. Eggs are a significant source of nutrition providing essentials nutrients like protein and choline to keep the human body healthy.

I never cease to be amazed at the wonders of nature! As the hen goes about her daily business her little body is constantly at work forming the next egg she will lay. The process of forming the egg, complete with shell and laying it takes around 24 hours. How does the hen do it? The process starts with the hen's eye. A light cue from either natural or artificial light stimulates a photo-receptive gland near the hen's eye to trigger the hormonal activity that allows us to have this amazing food.

To give you an appreciation of how awesome this process is and how the hens little body functions, I will now try in simple terms to give a description of what happens.

Firstly, a clutch of eggs, about 8 to13 egg yolks are forming simultaneously within the hen's body, but each one at a different stage of development. They grow to an optimum size according to the age of the hen and once that stage is reached hormonal activity releases the biggest yolk.

9 Developing Egg yolks

For the next 22 to 24 hours the work of making the remaining components of the egg takes place. The chalazae cords are attached to the yolk. These cords help keep the yolk centered in the albumen. The albumen itself is placed around the yolk in a spinning activity and is followed by the formation of the membrane which encompasses the white and yolk. Once this stage is completed, in response to recognising that the egg needs to be plumped up to form a firm base on which to lay down the shell the hens body creates a watery white which fills out the membrane making it ready for shelling. Shell formation itself takes up to 20 to 22 hours. If we look at the shell under a microscope, we discover that it consists of layers and layers of tiny spheres, each one individually made of pure calcium and placed on the egg to make natures very own protective wrapping. Once her body realizes that the shell is complete, she then places the color, and a protective varnish called the cuticle on the shell.

Sometimes we get queries from customers about certain flaws in the egg. Well as you can see from the above activity the formation of eggs is ongoing. Should the hen get a fright or come under any stress while the egg is forming it is only natural to expect that flaws may appear. Some of these flaws will be on the inside of the egg and may not be detected before reaching the consumer. A fairly typical one is known as a blood spot, meat spot or blood splash. This is generally due to the hen getting some sort of fright which causes her body to jerk or contract. During this sudden movement a blood vessel can rupture, and the blood released gets wrapped up in the forming egg. At what location within the egg, the extraneous matter appears is determined by what stage of development the egg was at when the fright occurred.

The yolk color is largely influenced by the hen's diet. Most of the nutrients are in the yolk but the albumen is a very rich source of protein which is easily absorbed by the human body. The larger end of the egg contains an air cell which forms as the egg cools down after it's been laid. As the egg gets older the air space increases in size due to the exchange of moisture and gasses through the pores on the shell. As the size of the air cell increases, the quality and weight of the egg is also affected. This is why the albumen in an older egg is less viscous than that of a fresher egg. It also accounts for why a fresh egg will sink to the bottom if dropped into a glass of water while an older egg will float. The older the eggs the higher it will suspend in the water.

It is amazing to me how one simple egg can provide so much in terms of nutrients.

We are governed by the Department of Agriculture, Food and the Marine and under European Union Egg Marketing regulations we must hold an up to date Packing License. Our original packing system was manually based and could only pack 5 cases (1800 eggs) an hour, but in the early 1990's we upgraded and were able to pack up to 27 cases (9720 eggs) an hour. An automatic America stainless steel, Diamond Grader, was purchased in 2001 enabling us to pack up to 100 cases (36,000 eggs) per hour.

While there may have been times that we struggled to meet demand as our customer base grew, we were confident that our product was always fresh and of the highest quality. We were keen to do the thing properly, keeping the quality of our product as a top priority.

Through all this growth and positive developments, our family endured two of life's biggest upheavals. So, it is fair to say that the upgrading referred to above and the changes to our business model at the end of the 90's and early 2000, while desirable for quite some time were made out of necessity rather than desire.

The Loss of Our Matriarch

There is an old saying, "It takes a village to rear a child", and a truer word has never been said. The children were good, but by no means angels. They were more curious than troublemakers. Trying to keep an eye on four young children with an age gap of 6 years between the oldest and youngest, maintain the farm and run a business, myself and Leo were certainly put through our paces. Thankfully, we had the invaluable support of our families.

Mammy was a pillar of support to us, helping by minding the children, or keeping on top of the housework, or even just arriving for a visit with freshly baked bread and maybe even a jar of homemade damson jam. Unfortunately, Mammy hadn't been well, and in 1995, she was diagnosed with acromegaly. This meant she had an overactive pituitary gland, which was releasing growth hormone that caused her feet, hands, and lower jawbone to grow. The pituitary gland needed to be removed. She had her surgery in early 1995, and follow-up scans showed an aneurism in her brain. This would require more surgery. Dr. Pidgeon, whom we knew already from when my sister Mary's brain trauma, was Mammy's neurosurgeon.

In October 1995, Mammy had her first aneurism corrected, but still required a second operation, which was scheduled for June 1996. Two weeks beforehand, myself and Mammy went to Lourdes on the annual diocesan pilgrimage. It was an enjoyable trip that offered reassurance to us both ahead of her surgery.

We knew that there was a 50/50 chance this would not have a good outcome, but Mammy's strong trust in God meant that she believed He would see her through this operation, just as He had with the first surgery the previous year.

This time the operation did not go as well as we all had hoped and unfortunately, she was unable to communicate for the rest of her life.

For the last four years of her life, she was unable to live independently, so we found her a place in a nursing home, the same nursing home that had cared for Mary towards the end of her illness. It was a difficult time adjusting to the changes that this brought, especially the massive difference in my support structure. Instead of focusing on the difficulties, we surrounded her with family and as much love as we possibly could during those years before she passed away in October 2000.

The Accident and My Changing Role

As mammy's recovery lay in the balance, and my siblings and I along with daddy were trying to decide on the best future care for mammy, we were faced with further challenges. In August 1996, a mere two months after Mammy's surgery, Leo had an accident on his way to deliver eggs in Dublin. Six miles from home, he was involved in a head-on collision with a fully-loaded milk tanker. He suffered massive injuries including internal bleeding. He lost an eye, but his main injury was damage to his liver and for 10 days his life hung in the balance. Suddenly, I was taken from the driver's seat of our business to a bedside vigil, praying that my best friend and father of my kids wouldn't leave us. My brain was whirling. I had the children to care for, my mother's health issues and of course, the business. How was I going to keep all those balls in the air without Leo's steadying hand at my side? We were a team and I felt devastated at the possible loss of my teammate, partner and friend.

Many of us have dealt with tragic events in our lives, but there are moments when your life comes into crystal clear focus. I prayed a lot in those days, asking God for strength for myself and healing for Leo. My faith was a light during this dark time, and I relied heavily on it and on God to see me through. One thing I remember clearly, was asking God not to leave Leo with us if he was going to need full time care. I think the accident and Leo's condition awakened a selfish streak in me.

I felt that I didn't have what it took to mind someone who's every need became my responsibility.

Fortunately, less than a year beforehand, we had hired our first employee, Alison. She is still with us today, but during that time, it was clear that she was an answer to prayer. Alison had come to us on a temporary contract; to set up a good filing system. We saw the value in having someone who could dedicate to the business and decided to offer her fulltime work when the filing contract ran out. She became a key person in the business and in 1995 she helped to set up our first quality control system. At the time of the accident, Alison was only 20, and already was like part of the family. She stepped into my shoes, managing the business in my absence. She stayed at night, minding the children and making sure they had a hot dinner if I wasn't there to cook myself, and when I'd get home, she was there waiting with a cup of tea to offer a listening ear. She was such a crucial support for me, our children, and our business.

Alison had a fantastic attention to detail, which meant that nothing fell through the cracks. Sometimes I still wonder just how she did it, because we didn't miss a delivery and met all the commitments made to our suppliers and customers alike.

It was an unsettling time for the four children, but between Alison's care and the help of their aunts, uncles and cousins who brought them on holiday and minded them in the weeks running up to their return to school, we had enough support to tackle the new challenges head on. By late September, Leo was home from hospital, but his movements were limited, and he could walk only with the support of a walking frame. Inevitably, this meant that he couldn't move at the same speed he was used to. Recovery was going to take time. My brothers and their wives not only helped with the children, but also with our parents. I cannot thank them enough for their support in this time, as it allowed me to balance caring for Leo and visiting Mammy, while juggling the other aspects of our lives that needed my attention.

We tried not to tell mammy about Leo's accident, as her own health was fragile, but she found out anyway from another patient. I had to go and tell her about the accident and assure her that Leo would be okay, even though I was not at all certain myself at the time. "Mammy, you know me very well, yeah? You know how I would not be able to pretend about anything so serious as this. So, when I speak to you about Leo, you know I will tell you the truth." This approach appeased her, as she trusted me fully and her concerns were alleviated to some degree at least; although it may have been one of the few times in my life that Mammy wasn't able to see my own doubts. Leo was like another son to her, so I knew that to tell her the full truth about his condition would have devastated her, particularly when she was unable to communicate her thoughts or feelings. I will never ever forget her joy and elation when he was able to make the first visit with her. She clapped her hands and screamed with delight. Even now I shed a tear remembering that bittersweet, joyful event. Then we realized just how aware mammy still was of her surroundings and how she could understand things even though she was unable to communicate.

Throughout all of these events and my own anger, I realized how truly forgiving and compassionate God is. Leo made a full recovery and although he is not without pain, he doesn't complain, and we are both grateful for all that we have, but especially each other.

Overall, our lives haven't changed that much, we plan special holidays and splurge on a new car for Leo now and again, but other than that, we keep our lives modest and focused on our family. Life has brought challenges, but we have met them successfully with God's help.

*Leo (first big outing 1yr after the accident)
with the children in Croke Park 1997*

Moving Forward

The 2000s were to take on a more uplifting tone, as we were expanding the packing center, the business was doing well and continuing to grow, the children were growing up, and Leo was well. In early 2001, we received a request to provide an Omega-3 enriched egg to the market, which is achieved by introducing specific ingredients into the hens' diet. We investigated the possibility and swiftly returned to our customer with a proposal.

Part of our research was finding the right guidance, so we could introduce the omega-3 enrichment in the best way. While many competitors use fish oils to achieve an enriched egg, we have found that it is easier and more sustainable to give the hens seaweed as part of their feed. The result is that by using measured quantities in their feed, we can measure the enrichment that is transferred to the eggs themselves. Our research quickly yielded results and our enriched egg offering was on the supermarket shelf within 6 months.

New grading facility & equipment 2001

While Leo is still very much part of our business, as time went on, it was clear that I was going to have to take on an even greater leadership role. Remember my need to stand out without sticking out? I was now in the position where I had to take on the business and stick my neck out. I couldn't be timid with my family's livelihood on the line. I struggled for so long, just wanting to blend in, particularly when it came to making presentations for our company. Yet it was one of those presentations that actually helped me to find my voice and a greater level of confidence in my own expertise.

In 2005, one of our customers put their business out to tender in the form of an "e-auction," a concept that was nearly alien to us up until that point. The first step in this new process was to bid for the supply value of their business and later on in the tendering process, we were required to make a presentation to the client, outlining our processes and answering questions about our operations. Through a friend, I met a wonderful individual who works with those preparing to make major presentations. I wanted to hire her to make our presentation, but she kept reminding me, "Nobody can tell the story of your company and your products like you can." She had a reassuring positive for every negative that came to my mind. That first presentation went surprisingly well. I was prepared and knew my topic, and it showed to my audience. My nerves may have been all over the place, but nobody knew that but me.

That presentation changed my outlook and worked wonders for my confidence level. I finally recognized that I was the expert, and my audience was seeking information from me. It was a heady feeling, and I now find public speaking and communicating with others much easier because I realize that when you know your topic well, it gives you a confidence boost and your audience truly associates you with expert status.

Expanding Our Business and Building a Charity Partnership

We have always tried to make our mark through innovation and in 2008, we had an idea to introduce a product to the Irish market that was not already available, "white shelled eggs".

I am about to share a fact with you that the average egg loving consumer does not know. If you want to have white eggs, you need white hens with pale earlobes.

During this time period, we were trying to think of an alternative marketing plan to create market presence for this new offering and make it stand out. When picking out the packaging, we wanted a colour that was not already present on the shop shelf. After seeing the pink pack, we couldn't help but think this was the best pack for our white eggs. During the further design stages, the idea of partnering with a charity was proposed, and we loved the idea and embraced it.

As you may have realized, cancer research was close to our hearts due to both our family's long history with the disease. I couldn't help but be reminded of my own sister and Leo's mother as we prepared to make our first contribution. Our faith had helped us through those losses, but it also gave us the courage to help others whose loved ones were struggling with this disease. It didn't take long for us to decide on the charity we would like to work with and approached Action Breast Cancer about a partnership. This meant that we would be allowed to use the pink ribbon on the packaging and eggs and a portion of the money from all the eggs sold from this line was given to the charity.

Over the years, we have changed to a different cancer charity, but the idea of giving back has continued to be part of our white eggs sales. Our employees have also gotten involved and it has truly become a company endeavor.

Changes in Regulations

In the early 1990s, the EU banned conventional cages, although the ban was only due to come into effect on January 1st, 2012. While the industry was pushing for instructions on their new production systems, we saw an opportunity to step in and grow our business. See, we realized that Free Range and the welfare of the birds were of increasing importance to the customer and consumer alike. There was a natural growth in Free Range and this all meant that we had decisions to make. Either we stay as we are, or we push for growth. I'm not going to lie. This wasn't a labored decision. Leo and I have similar beliefs in terms of our business and in this situation, we both agreed that to stay the same would equate to pedaling backwards.

The decision to continue growing the company could have consequences, which created the challenge of surplus. One thing that had become innately clear in the years that we had been developing our business was that the free-range customer had definitive preference for large eggs. This creates a problem in terms of growth as normal hen production results in similar quantities of medium and large eggs on average over the course of the flock's life cycle, but the time it takes for flocks to reach the stage of laying large eggs must also be considered. To continue growing the business, we could not always rely on increased sales, as this would likely exacerbate the problem presented by having a greater volume of surplus in the smaller sizes. We had to devise a plan for the long term, thinking laterally and strategically.

The above challenges in experiencing growth and with a ban on traditional cages to come into effect in 2012, we anticipated the urgent need to prepare ourselves. Now, as you remember, I told you earlier that we were a dedicated Free-Range Egg producer and packer, so you may ask, "Why would a ban on traditional cages effect dedicated free range?"

An extra little bit of history in this regard is needed. The European commission introduced the ban on traditional cages in 1999 but given the number of caged units in Europe the changeover period was always going to span years, and the powers that be decided on a deadline of the 1st January 2012. It has largely faded from memory now, but the discussions around cage production in the late 90's always made us feel like it wasn't going to be a simple time. Time progressed and some countries within Europe were progressive in the changeover, but there were others that lagged behind, perhaps not believing that the deadlines would be so strict. We knew the consumer was growing ever more aware of animal welfare, so for the industry to miss this deadline was not going to be tolerated.

This had been such a hot topic at the turn of the century we instinctively knew that there would be a revival of the discussion in the media.

The duration of the 00's was relatively calm, where welfare groups patiently respected the grace period allowed by legislatures. For many it was business as usual, for us the noughties meant watching, assessing, learning, interpreting and projecting. By 2003, we had the idea of growing from the core, using the knowledge we had but learning new skills and applying them by starting to process eggs. For a few years, this was merely an idea, one that became a dream that occupied many hours of our waking and working time. I must say that luck was on our side, because a series of chance encounters at various events led us to the Fusion Graduate Program. We started this program in 2007, with the hiring the first Graduate, Roberto. Roberto was tasked with researching the market for potential egg products, along with methods of processing. Lasting 2 years, the program allowed us to team up with a college helping us to gain expertise in an unknown field within industry while giving the graduate themselves real world business experience. This was an invaluable opportunity for us, widening our horizons and making the ideas we had for our future tangible. While Roberto researched the options available to us, every morsel of information was absorbed in an attempt to arm ourselves with the knowledge needed to know when to dive in with this new venture.

While this period was long awaited and took great patience, we felt we were still too small to sacrifice the core business by moving too soon. Timing needed to be perfect, the ability to process surplus eggs would negate most of the economic pressures of growing supply, but to grow too soon the investment could be lost and could have the opposite effect. By 2011 the cage side of the industry was really starting to gear up to the change in legislation. This was the time to take the leap, we sought premises, ordered our equipment (all of which was new, verging on bespoke for our requirements) and we were in full action by mid-2012. Only time would tell if our judgement had been correct.

How could we have surplus eggs? Primarily, as we would increase our production our volume of eggs that would not be saleable on the retail market would increase in either small eggs, too big eggs or indeed slight misfits. As part of the grading process, not every egg can be packed and shipped, because they didn't meet the various required grading standards. There is nothing wrong with these eggs, but they would have to be sold for low returns so we set about finding a way to use these eggs, a way that would be more economically wise for a small company. We did our homework, made our application and became part of the Fusion program.

The University of Ulster, Coleraine became our "knowledge partner" offering us expertise in many areas of our research. The program lasted two years where we interacted with the college on market research, food production and testing and guidance on sourcing suitable equipment. So back to Roberto, our graduate who joined us in August 2007. Prior to Roberto's selection as the suitable candidate, I prayed that the graduate would be the right person for our company, and I could not have imagined how completely this prayer was answered. At interview, Roberto spoke about his passion for food with such conviction that he far surpassed all competition. His family owned their own business in Puebla, Mexico, so he had a huge understanding of what working in a small family owned business entailed. We literally had no idea then how much he would become part of our family throughout the following years. With his new skillsets, our horizons were opened.

Today, this operation has grown into a successful business in its own right and is set to be a big part of our future growth as we tap into the expanding demand for sources of protein for sports enthusiasts, pregnant women, young children, and the elderly.

Roberto's expertise allowed us to go the route of breaking the surplus eggs and pasteurizing them. Along the way, I was able to travel to the United States three times to get more information and research ideas. Visits to Europe were also great opportunities to network and do research. The Fusion program came to an end in 2009, so we had to decide what we were going to invest in and make our own reality. Pasteurizing seemed the way to go but it took another 3 years to realise the dream. Understand that this meant a huge investment, in terms of deposits, securing a location and then finding possible customers willing to try our new products.

The separation step in the breaking & pasteurising process

Production of pasteurized products started on last day of June 2012. Doing small quantities at first, we were able to test demand and become very adept at understanding the new process and the new product specifications.

Not in our wildest dreams could we have imagined where the journey that began with 150 hens would lead. We now have 20 farms supplying us in addition to our own hens, and 35 employees. Our oldest child, AnneMarie is living and working in Australia, and her 3 siblings are employed in the family business.

From Eggs to Little Chicks

Nature provides her very own packaging for the egg. As the eggshell is considered a reproductive chamber, the shell is constructed to protect a growing chick, in a fertilized egg, for the 21 days incubation period. Hens will lay eggs whether there is a male (rooster) present or not, but eggs will only be fertilized if there is interaction between males and females. Eggs for hatching is a different type of poultry enterprise and as we do not have any males with our hens there is absolutely no chance that our eggs are fertilized. Remember I mentioned earlier that a clutch of eggs is between 8 and 13 and they are positioned inside the hen's body like a bunch of grapes. They will be laid on consecutive days and then the hen will take a rest before either beginning a new clutch or if she is in the wild, she will become broody to hatch out the clutch just laid. Different farming systems specialize in the different areas of production and so while our specialty is to produce table eggs for human consumption others engage in producing eggs for hatching and again others specialize in rearing the little chicks from day old to maturity.

Fertilized eggs will begin to form the little embryo once the correct temperature for incubation and cell development has been reached. In these modern times this process takes place at big hatcheries where huge incubators simulate the special conditions provided in nature by the female bird. The conditions required change as the embryo develops and require specific levels of heat and humidity. Inside the egg nature has provided everything the growing chick needs. The yolk is the food that nourishes the little chick through the 21 days incubation. The albumen both provides protection in terms of a barrier in early development and protein for the developing tissues throughout incubation.

The shell protects the growing chick and when the time arrives for the little chicken to peck its way into the world it is positioned within the shell so that its little head is at the wide end close to the air space which provides it with its first intake of air. The shell too has been providing nutrition during the incubation and thus has weakened so that the little one can break through easily. Calcium from the shell has been transferred to the developing bones of the chick and also to its beak where an egg tooth has formed on the little beak for the purpose of cracking the shell.

Isn't nature just so amazing to provide for all these needs!

In the wild a female will lay all her clutch over consecutive days but another amazing fact is that while the eggs range in age at the time of incubation the chicks will actually hatch out within hours of one another. This is because the female only spends the minimum of time on the nest while she lays the eggs. Then when the last egg in the clutch is laid, she sits for longer raising the temperature of all the eggs to synchronize cell division. The heat and moisture generated by her body provides the optimum conditions for her brood.

To have a successful hatch she will continuously turn the eggs so as to allow them all to develop at the same rate. When they develop to a certain stage withing the shell she communicates with them and they communicate not only back with her but with one another prior to hatching. This is how she learns the sound of each of their little voices and she is ready to protect them when they are running around. Once they all hatch out, she takes them on various adventures, and she uses a process called "imprinting" to teach them all they need to know about living and how to survive.

CHAPTER THREE

The Modest Little Hen

Our family home and packing plant is located on a hill in what is known locally as Drumlin country. The grassy fields used as hens' paddocks are hilly too, and our two hen houses are located in the middle of the paddocks allowing almost 360° access to the hens. An avenue for access runs parallel to a natural hedge.

I will never tire of the wonderful sight of our flocks of white and brown hens happily scratching and scraping across those fields, all visible in their large numbers due to the sloping terrain. I marvel at how these little creatures, sometimes are regarded as humble, often considered stupid, profoundly dumb and underestimated so often, because after all the production of an egg almost on a daily basis for them is no big deal!

Well, if you think that about these little feathered ones you are widely off the mark!

These modest little creatures have so much to boast about, nor indeed are they stupid or dumb as is sometimes believed. I would prefer to substitute shy and reserved for stupid and dumb but believe me these little ones have personality. For sure what you see is not what you get, but I can happily grant full pardon to any reader who has regarded the hen as stupid and the production of an egg as simple if you allow me in return to indulge a while in talking up the achievements of these cautious but extremely inquisitive little creatures.

A young hen will begin laying at anything from 18 to 21 weeks. Nature provides for the hen to lay in cycles with the first cycle being the most productive, laying 6 eggs a week for many weeks in that cycle. Next time you hold a carton of 6 eggs in your hand consider that you have the equivalent of one week's produce from a hen before you and those 6 eggs are a significant fraction of the weight of the hen that produced them. A hen will lay about 530 eggs in a lifetime, but the production rate tapers off as the hen ages. Typically, just over 70% will be laid in the first cycle but once the hen reaches the age of natural molt her ability to make a really good shell that protects the contents is reduced along with her rate of lay.

The ovary and oviduct are the reproductive system of the hen and it takes a hen about 24 hours to produce an egg. Then, after laying today's egg the hen's metabolism will stall for about 40 minutes before another yoke is released from the ovary.

The ovary is located just under the hens' backbone about midway between the neck and tail and can contain several thousand ova. As the hen reaches maturity these ova develop a few at a time into yokes. The yoke is completely formed in the ovary from where it is released as soon as the follicle in which it is contained, ruptures.

Now the daily journey begins! The oviduct receives the yoke from the ovary and straight away the production of the remaining parts of the egg begins as the yoke makes its way naturally along this tube-like organ. Chalazae, albumen, shell membrane and eventually the shell itself are formed as the egg passes along its 25inch [625mm] journey approx., before it is ready for discharge. The egg on its journey will have acquired its shell color as it journeys through the oviduct, pointed side first. Then almost at the point of laying, the egg does a 180-degree turn. Now the egg is about to be introduced to the world, blunt end first. Why? Well, it is all in the interest of hygiene, isn't it; the little stupid, dumb chicken had it worked out before the intelligent human who had to research why, and when we did, we learned that the little hen wants the expulsion of the egg to be rapid, so as to eliminate the risk of inward infection.

Chalaza is the two twisted membrane strings that holds the yoke centered in the albumen, the strong egg white that surrounds the yolk. Together with the yoke these constituent parts are enclosed in the shell membrane before being encased in the calcium shell, and all in a days' work for the hen. When the membrane encapsulates its contents initially it is a bit floppy but one of the wonders of nature identifies that this would not be a sound foundation to form a strong and perfect shell so at that point the capsule is plumped up with a watery substance to become firm and the process of laying down the shell takes place. The membrane itself is made up of protein called collagen which is a really precious and expensive material often used in the making of many face creams.

Now is there anything simple, stupid or dumb about that!

Some readers may say that this process has evolved over many millions of years, and that is true of course; true for us too as humans, because once back in time we were pretty basic ourselves. Over millennia though, through spoken word, manuscripts, multiple learning processes and now the internet, we have become the very superior form of Earth's species. Remember that we were chosen to inhabit the Earth in God's image and likeness, so we had an advantage from the beginning of life on Earth, but thumbs up to the little hen, she has done rather well too, I think.

I am fascinated with the hen and not just because she is our farms source of income. The hen is a feeding, walking, scratching, perching, sleeping, nutritious food factory, that manages to provide one of nature's wrapping on her finished product. Not only that but in today's world its "wow" factor is there is absolutely no waste if we the consumer were only a fraction as clever as the hen herself.

Whenever you use an egg, you need to break the shell.

That shell is also created; start to finish within the time that the yoke is released from the ovary into a 26/25-inch journey through the oviduct, via a fascinating natural process. Consumers throw eggshells away, but it is a costly part of any egg for the hen to produce. The shell provides a most important barrier between the perfect nutritious contents within it and an open environment where bacteria, viruses and pathogens might roam.

Scientists have known and understood the structure of the eggshell for well over a century.

I often stroll through our hens and as I do I get the impression that they want to know more about me too; they come up close and now and then one presents herself for a cuddle, but most approach slowly on their inwardly hinged knees, turning their heads right to left all the time, curious to explore a bit about me while always watching behind them. Over the years I regularly felt the need to respond to this call for a cuddle so I would pick her up and chat a little; "Can you tell me where you get the stuff that makes your shell?" I am so animated by their presence, but not mad enough to expect an answer. So, I determined to learn more about my beautiful endearing feathered companions. In 2011, I signed up for an Applied Poultry Science program at the Scottish Agriculture College in Ayr to learn all I could and understand more about my little friends.

So now I'll tell you a little about the formation of the eggshell.

Egg shells are formed by a process similar to how bone and seashells are formed. The yoke, the chalazae and the albumen are contained within the egg membranes. It is probably more accurate to attribute the formation of the shell to the egg itself than to the hen, but I personally prefer to give the credit to the hen. The egg membrane is very soft, and on its surface, it has a large number of equally spaced points. Clusters of calcite knobs adhere to these points, side by side initially in the first stage of shell formation. From these stacks the second layer of the shell; the palisade layer develops and finally a third thin outer layer called the cuticle completes the formation of the eggshell. The entire process takes over 20 hours and occurs simultaneous to the egg making its passage along the oviduct. The colour of the shell is determined also during this journey.

A typical eggshell is made up of 97% calcium carbonate. The calcium has to be provided as part of the hens' diet, broken down in the small intestine and absorbed into the blood stream, then transferred either to the bones or directly to the shell gland for storage until released whenever required to form the egg shell. The carbonate is produced naturally by the hens' complex metabolism. When an eggshell is being laid down by the hen, stored calcium is secreted into the blood system and deposited on the egg membrane in tiny molecules. Approximately 2.3 grams of calcium will be released by the hen to produce every shell and bearing in mind that this occurs up to 6 times in one week it is quite an extraordinary feat for the hen. The finished eggshell, while appearing smooth to the naked eye is quite a structure under the microscope. There are up to 17,000 pores in the shell of a normal egg, formed because the calcium carbonate deposits are spherical in shape. The shell measures only between 0.24 – 0.41mm in thickness yet it is amazingly strong and is capable of withstanding over 100lbs (45.4 kgs) of pressure when compressed from both ends.

Laying hens will very often reduce egg production as the days shorten, and their bodies begin to molt, that is; lose the old feathers and grows a whole new plumage. Typically, hens have 8000 feathers, but that number can vary greatly.

There are three major feather types on hens; Down, Contour and Flight feathers, but hens can fly short distances only, as they have a narrow wingspan and a large body mass compared to wild fowl or Nature's birds of flight. The hen's feathers have other uses though like providing insulation and retaining body heat, providing a means of communicating through flapping and fluffing, providing a way of attracting a mate and of course assisting in the limited flight referred to earlier.

During molting as old feathers fall off, new ones are produced by follicles in the skin. Each feather is made up almost entirely from keratin, so is the hens' beak and claws, and incidentally keratin makes up our own nails and hair. However, feathers unlike our hair will stop growing when they reach the right length.

Across a hen's back an iridescent green sheen may often be seen particularly on dark plumage. This sheen is highly desirable in show birds and is often regarded as a sign of a healthy bird. This iridescence is frequently used in courtship displays, so it can add vanity to the hens' profile too.

Hens will consume about half a cupful (135gms approx.) of balanced cereal food per day and they will pick up more while roaming in the pastures. They will normally lay their eggs in the morning hours. Each eggs arrival is followed by a period of cackling which can last up to 15 minutes. This is in stark contrast, a mother hen's "cluck" conversing with the little brood which is distinctly different from the "cackling" which announces that she just laid an egg. It is believed that the reason for cackling is to draw predators away from the site of the nest. When you consider that hens originated as Jungle fowl it is quite a reasonable and believable theory. Immediately after laying each egg the hen makes her way to the drinker to consume much needed water. They do not have a tongue to help with drinking so this exercise is managed by filling their mouth from a water drinker and raising their heads to the sky until the water is transferred to their stomach by gravity. They are quite intelligent, contrary to common belief. Research continues in this area and studies have already discovered that hens can count, or at least be attracted to the larger of two volumes of feedstuff or anything else to their liking. They have shown levels of self-awareness and can even be manipulative.

They are incredibly clean also. Several times a daily they will be found "dustbathing". They do this by scratching a hollow in the field or in the designated "scratch area" which we provide them with a fresh supply of dry sand for this purpose. They almost bury themselves in the loose material flicking it into their feathers with their wings and feet. Once this part is complete, they will then "preen" their feathers. This is to settle the feathers back neatly on their bodies and make themselves look attractive. They do this using their beak and the preen gland which is positioned just where the tail and back meet. The preen gland produces oil and the hen using her beak squeezes at the gland, releasing the natural oils to polish her feathers and then arranges them as nature designed. This explains too why the feathers always look shiny.

Surprised?

Well, I'm no longer surprised. Every day they teach me more and more and I am continuously saying just how truly amazing this little creature of nature actually is!

Over the years a number of hens with character and attitude have come our way on the farm, but I am confining my descriptions to three that made their mark in different ways; Tweeny: The Bantam, Wonder woman: Diana and Miss Cheeky: An Escapee.

Tweeny, The Bantam:

The little Bantam hen, Tweeny came to us with a few other normal sized hens when a family member was getting out of poultry and looking for a good home for their little flock. The bantam is about half the size of a normal hen and is more ornamental that productive. She settled in and paraded about the yard as if she was the boss. Each evening the hens came back to the henhouse at nightfall and once they were inside, we closed them in for the night. One morning, carrying out my daily routine I arrived at the hen house to feed the flock and discovered Tweeny was missing: the darn fox, I thought, must have got her yesterday but fingers crossed she may turn up. Days passed and no sign of Tweeny, so I resigned myself that she was gone. Then one morning to my great surprise when I turned up with the feed, she appeared from behind a box that was sitting angle-wise in the corner. When I checked she had two eggs and I figured she was trying to hatch chicks.

A fertilised egg takes 21 days to hatch and during that time the broody hen will sit for endless hours keeping the temperature of the egg at an optimum level to ensure a healthy chick when hatched. For the first few days she may not leave the nest at all. As the little chick develops within the egg it cheeps and chirrups and the hen will respond so by the time the little one hatches out, they already know one another, and the multiple chicks also are familiar with one another. Anyway, back to Tweeny and her two eggs.

Well given that she had no partner she was going to be disappointed and perhaps being a mother already myself I felt sad for her, after all she would spend days waiting and have nothing for her time. I expressed this to Leo who immediately said "Why don't you call Elmbank Hatchery, in Cavan and order half dozen day old chicks. We can slip them under her one night after dark and she will bond with them." Well, this was my introduction to one of nature's miracles. Days later we received our 6 tiny yellow balls of fluff chirping delightfully in a luxuriously lined cardboard box with holes around the sides to allow the air to circulate inside.

That night we carried out step 2 of the plan and that too worked magically. Instantly when Tweeny heard the chirruping, she clucked away herself and so a conversation began. Next morning, she emerged from her nest behind the box, but it was too tall for the babies. She would not go near the food for herself without them and kept returning to the corner calling them. I'm sure you are aware that if a human touches a bird's nest before the young are hatched the bird will abandon the nest and so we were anxious to avoid any interference until the new family had bonded.

Well watching the antics of the new mother, she was not going anywhere without her little ones so once the other hens had fed and left the hen house, we lifted the box and allowed the 6 little ones reunite with mum. Their very first taste of freedom.

We had already penned off a section in the henhouse for them that they could be separate from the other hens and establish their own behaviors. The other hens were not terribly bothered by the new arrivals. I often wonder what might have happened if any of them had been broody. Would they try to kidnap some of the baby chicks?

We had, in the past instances on the farm where a cow was very receptive to adopting another cow's calf when that one's mother died. This happened too with our dogs where one new mother absolutely insisted on taking a puppy for another's litter.

Well back to Tweeny and her brood, we provided a supply of chick mash, the special feed for new hatchlings and water. On day one and even day two very little food was consumed. It appeared to be just scratched all over the place making a rather messy bed. We were concerned that they would go hungry but in fact we need not have worried. I have since learned that the chick within the shell while preparing to emerge into the world it consumes the egg yolk which is nature's way of providing sufficient nutrients for a couple of days and so on those first few days they learn to scratch and peck.

In the days that followed we gave them access to wider areas and as mother and her chicks became more and more familiar with their surroundings they travelled further afield.

The days turned into weeks the chicks grew bigger than the mammy. That was quite funny really as she continued to protect them. She could be heard calling and calling, and we could even detect panic if one ran off into the long grass or went temporally missing. Her body language spoke volumes too and it became very obvious when she was angry with one or more of the broods.

I have a lasting memory of the sound of her voice as she expressed frustration one evening when they returned to the henhouse after the days adventure and she wanted them to perch up high in the rafters. Easy for her she was a tiny bird and could fly quite high but you will have learned earlier that the hen's ability to fly is limited due to the ratio of wing strength and body weight and so they were could only perch lower down. Well, she gave out and gave out but by now they were typical teenagers and were just about to be less dependent on the doting mom.

Diana, Wonder Woman:

Back in the early days when we were allowed mix different ages of birds, on one occasion, we discovered a young hen with a twisted beak. Our children were small at the time. One day while in the hen house AnneMarie spotted this bird coming from the perches after the others were finished feeding and had headed off to the paddocks. She watched and when the bird began feeding, she noticed the deformity. When we checked this was not a fresh injury, if in fact an injury at all and it was very obvious that this bright lady had found her place in the hierarchy and was managing very well.

When the rest of the flock moved outside each day she saw the opportunity to attend at the feeder without being bullied. It appeared to us that at some point in her rearing she had an accident and incurred a broken jaw or perhaps she might even have been born that way. We segregated her for a while to establish if she was able to eat enough meal and learned that not only was she able to eat sufficient meal to maintain a lovely body shape and feathering but she laid a beautiful brown, well shelled medium egg every day. As flocks get older and disease risk increases, we must clear out the flock and restock with new hens. Well, this little wonder bird, we called her Diana after wonder woman, managed to survive through 3 different culls but in the end as she was getting old, sadly we had to let her go.

Miss Cheeky, An Escapee:

Each day when we opened the pop holes allowing the birds access to the range one particular bird began an adventure trip. What we first noticed was that about midday every day a hen showed up on the yard seeking admittance to the henhouse. How she got there was the mystery?

After opening the pop holes one morning I returned to the yard sharply. Within a few minutes I noticed "Miss Cheeky" make her way on to a low roof which overhung the paddock at one point. After making a short flight on to a higher roof she stepped her way up the ridge on the back of the granary to the apex of the building. The granary is a building adjacent to both the yard and the paddocks. From her lofty perch she now had a "birds eye view" all around the farmyard and the paddocks.

Next, she stepped on to the apex and travelled sideways the full length of the building making her way down the ridge on the front of and opposite end of the building. Here a pipe carrying water was suspended between two buildings, crossed over the yard. She proceeded to go on to the pipe which was quite flexible and made a swinging motion as she landed on it.

When she reached the middle of the pipe, she settled for a moment eventually flying down on to the yard below. Now if that was not enough, she developed a determined gait stretching her neck perking up her tail, moving very fast in the direction of the road. We watched at a distance knowing that if she sensed that we were following she would change her plan specifically to mislead us. About 80 metres from our house and on the opposite side of the road she entered the hedge and disappeared. We simply could not find her.

About an hour later she was back at the yard seeking readmission. You will recall I mentioned earlier that hens are creatures of habit, well this routine continued until one day when it was extremely windy, she embarked on the journey.

As I watched her make her way along the apex of the granary with my heart in my mouth for fear she would get blown off the roof to her death I vowed that when she returned, I would curtail her activities from that day onwards.

Our poultry adviser in the early days once told us that if you clip a small bit off the long feathers on one wing only their flight will be unbalanced and so escaping is not as easy. That worked a treat in this case, and would you believe we never found her nest which proves that other theory also, that the cackling after laying is to mislead the predator.

It is an old saying also that "the hen that lays out once will do so continuously" so whether or not she settled for the luxurious nesting space we had provide we never knew. Only she herself and the good Lord knows the answer to that question.

CHAPTER FOUR

Free Range Eggs:
What Does It Mean?

Respecting all forms of life, and here I mean life in all ways that it is presented, surely would make for a better, more caring human race. I have already described how our hens are managed and lovingly looked after, so it will come as no surprise that we are not big fans of intensive farming.

Learning about keeping hens commercially while watching the amazing antics and that first flock of 150 hens settle and make Clonarn their home, indicated to us that the whole concept of mass production flew in the face of nature.

Thankfully, there has been a movement during the last few decades to step away from the big farming ideals, including caging hens, to get back to a more natural product. It's funny that our world has swung back toward those ideals and ways of doing things that were once considered old-fashioned. In many ways, we are realizing that we may have thrown the baby out with the bath water. Technology has allowed us to grade and pack our eggs, as well as find alternative uses for eggs that might be considered waste, but it still doesn't replace the care and connection of humans with their animals.

Throughout the ups and downs of our family's lives, we made the decision to treat our animals as if they were family. It meant giving them as much freedom as possible to wander and express their natural behaviors. The EU in 2012 banned all conventional cages for egg production, replacing them with much more animal friendly systems.

Here, I must pay a great complement to the consumer, our customer. If the consumer had not backed Free Range Egg production, there would have been no incentive to change the ways of production and the practice of producing eggs in battery cages might have continued unchallenged. While I fully understand that it is challenging to produce affordable food to feed the masses, I dislike any situation where natural behaviors of animals are restricted or limited. This belief stems from our childhood indoctrination of respect for all God's creatures. We cannot change who we are and so our love for traditional type Free Range production systems will always take priority over profits or compromise.

Free Range: An Ancient Farming Method

When I talk about free range, I'm referring to a type of animal husbandry that has been around for centuries. Here in Ireland, long before any type of wire fencing, herds of animals of all kinds and flocks of poultry were allowed to roam completely freely. Giving them their freedom allowed livestock to access a variety of vegetation and nutrients that enriched the flavor of the end product. Although around for a long time, Free range has resurged as a production means in the more recent past. Nowadays, the well-informed consumer with a few more cents to spend questions more and more where their food comes from, what is going into animal feed and how confinement affects the quality of life for the animals themselves.

In ancient Ireland, cattle were the primary source of wealth and status. These cows were allowed to feed on the open range. There was a custom called transhumance (in Ireland it was known as booleying), which was the seasonal movement of people and their livestock between summer and winter pasturage. Generally, the herds travel with attendants, but their owners stayed put with their crops. This transfer to the mountains during the summer alleviated pressure on the growing crops and provided fresh pasture. The practice was widespread in the west of Ireland up until the time of World War II.

Fences and county borders had an impact on this trend of free-range herds. As land was settled, people claimed land and defended it. Passage and grazing were no longer free, as drover trails became subject to regulations and even patrols. We began to fence our animals in and hens in cages became the "progressive" farming method for producing eggs. This type of production method also helped with the culture being developed all over the world of producing an affordable, nutritious product for the masses.

The return to the idea of animals with access to the outside and a life beyond a cage began to come back into vogue as organizations exposed the conditions that these animals sometimes faced. A new culture has developed which is propelled by a Generation of Millennials who are more decerning, have a growing love for nature and particularly for our food producing animals. The free range and organic movements continue to keep pressure on for more ethically produced food, giving greater consideration to the animals, while also addressing the issues of chemical exposure throughout our food chain.

Today, most countries have regulations to define what exactly can be considered free range. Farmers must adhere to the guidelines in order to label their products as free range. But that is not the case everywhere. In the next chapter, I'll talk more about the regulations that Irish eggs must conform to, but for now, let's talk about how other countries define free range.

When doing research for this book I was amazed to learn that in the United States, for example, the USDA free range regulations are basically non-existent. Currently, there is no specification for the length of time an animal spends outside, the quality or size of the outside range, just that the animal has access to the outside. In many cases, free range has become a marketing term and what constitutes free range is entirely up to the producer of the product, be it eggs or meat or even milk. At this point, it is a bit of a wild west in terms of regulations, but there are groups and individuals who are trying to get the USDA to produce a set of guidelines for labeling.

This is just one example of how the world is divided on the definition of free range. In many countries, it is "buyer beware" type of marketing. Others have attempted to regulate and provide consistent guidelines that producers must meet to call their products free range. For consumers, it is important to know the origin of and company providing your eggs, because depending on the country, those eggs could be subject to no regulation at all. However, Ireland has become a world leader in food production where the EU guidelines for egg production are further bolstered by the Irish Food bord's voluntary Sustainable Egg Assurance Scheme. Initially known as the Egg Quality Assurance Scheme was developed by Bord Bia in conjunction with the egg industry to look after the interests of the consumer and ensure the best life possible for the hens while they lay those delicious, nutritious eggs.

Margaret's Free Range

A strong belief in traditional type farming and a passion for our hens drives our ambition to produce the best eggs in Ireland. Our hens live in traditional type accommodation, enjoy plenty of fresh air, acres of green grass and to ensure they stay healthy we give them adequate quantities of quality feed daily. When we communicate that our hens are part of our family, it is not just words but a sincere characteristic born out of the love and appreciation for those first hens and their personalities which made a lifelong impression on all of us.

As I mentioned, even when it came to enriching our eggs, I looked for a more natural food option and found it in seaweed. Could we have just given them a supplement? These days, there is a supplement for everything. But by using a natural ingredient, we have achieved the results that we wanted and created a quality product for our consumers along with providing the hen with a better feed also. I wouldn't feed unhealthy food to the family, and so I could never imagine giving anything other than the best to the hens either.

Margaret having a little cuddle with a white hen

Our hens are part of the family

All our farms put the hen first. At Margaret's, we are a family of farmers who live and breathe what we do. The joy and satisfaction we feel from keeping hens, caring for the land, and producing eggs – the right way- is what inspires us and keeps us motivated to find ways to share a taste of that joy with the world.

Delivering an innovative range of free-range offerings from healthy, happy hens is more than a business – it's our passion. Our girls are simply part of our family, so we use time tested, traditional humane farming methods.

Giving them the freedom to forage expansive pastures of lush green grass, nourishing them with healthy natural feed and providing them with a continuous supply of fresh clean water allows us to give them a happy life. Keeping happy hens is what

we love and, in turn, it allows us to give something extraordinary
back to our community – the very best tasting egg there is.

This is not just rhetoric but a belief, a passion and the pillar our company is built on. All day long our hens can roam and graze freely in their dedicated pastures. Their comfortable housing provides protection from the elements at night along with the option to stroll in and out through the day they return for feed, drink and maybe a wee rest. Our houses are modern but of traditional design, as opposed to the very modern aviary type, tiered houses. Each house is kitted out with modern equipment enabling the hens to feed, drink and perch at will. They have access to specially designed nesting boxes with a slightly sloping floor which accommodates the safe removal of eggs from the space once the hen has her business completed. Two thirds of the floor space indoors is made of small slats which allows the hens dropping to fall into a pit and will only need removing at the end of the flock thus eliminating the need to disturb the hens at any time during their laying cycle. The other one third indoor floor space referred to as "the scratch area" is covered with dry sand and used by the hens to clean themselves, scratch and play and have shelter in the less clement outdoor weather.

Just like for us humans along with food, sleep and exercise is important for the hens too. The house has sufficient perching space for every bird, and this is where they sleep at night. Many hens sleep with their head tucked under their wing and look amazingly cosy. Roaming the paddocks provides the exercise needed to keep their bones strong, their lungs healthy, their eggs wholesome and their attitude sociable.

Keep in mind, our hens produce eggs that have a distinctive flavor. There is a belief that Happy hens lay great eggs: Well, I will go one step further and declare that it's the great outdoors that contribute mostly to the flavor. Of course, the hens are happy to have their freedom but hens that never have been outside do not know if they are missing out, so they are quite likely to be happy too. Our poultry adviser many years ago told us that providing fresh feed & clean water is a must, but the fresh air is more valuable than we could ever imagine in its contribution to the flavor.

Many times, over the past 30 years I've tried to place myself in the position of the hen. I for sure would not like to be confined in a small space every day but If I've never experienced otherwise how can I compare. Hens are naturally social creatures, so giving them the opportunity to interact with other creatures can have a positive impact on their overall wellbeing. Watching our hens interact with humans and with various other living creatures they encounter in the outdoors is such a joy. Even seeing how they socialize within their own hierarchical groupings is quite entertaining.

The hens, the eggs, the consumer, the farmer and the land all benefit from this freedom to come and go at will during daylight hours. I'm told that a hen will go to the paddock and back to the house about 30 times a day. Our experience in free range farming and the years of handed down "farming know-how" also contributes to a belief in what we do and the reason for committing to our chosen way of life. Users of our eggs constantly comment on "that" noticeable difference. "That" of course means different things for different people as some cook, some bake, some use in domestic settings and some in more commercial settings but each and all believe that the difference is a very positive one.

Organic or Free range now there's a question of the cryptic kind! In order to use the term Organic all inputs like pullet (pre-lay hen) feed and land must be Certified Organic with one of the registered Organic bodies. The use of chemicals is also prohibited. But under EU regulations it is not mandatory to give the hens access to the outdoors. Free range on the other hand must have access to the outdoors and this is why we had to use the term Barn a few years ago when we were instructed to keep our hens indoors due to the dangers of Avian Influenza to the health of the hens, while the Organic farmers did not need to make any change to their labelling. With regard to chemicals and Free range our policy is to only use of medicines or chemicals if prescribed by our veterinary supervisor. I cannot remember when we last need to take such action.

Our commitment to our customers and consumer continues to take precedence. Monthly we read about different types of food fraud and eggs are sometimes mentioned as misrepresented of wrongly dated. In an attempt to address this and give our ever-valued customers an above reproach product, two years ago we teamed up with a company called Oritain, bases in New Zealand. Oritain's technology can analyse food products raising a profile for the farm of origin, a type of DNA or fingerprinting. This scientific breakthrough enables us to verify product origin thus offering a beyond doubt guarantee of authenticity to our consumers. Margaret's is the only egg in Western Europe giving this guarantee.

Bord Bia Sustainable Egg Assurance Scheme (SEAS)

About 80% of the eggs in the ROI are produced under the Bord Bia Sustainable Egg Assurance Scheme. This is a voluntary scheme, where membership demands high levels of compliance with the Standard or Code of Practice. The scheme covers both production and packing of eggs. While this is a voluntary scheme, accreditation to the scheme is required before being accepted as a supplier to most major customers, like retailers and many food service providers. Prospective members must firstly be registered with the Irish Department of Agriculture, Food and the Marine before making application to become a member. Initially an intensive Audit of the farm or packing center will take place and certification to the scheme will only take place when all aspects of the standard are met. Continued membership depends on full compliance at all audits thereafter. On farm inspections are carried out monthly on behalf of Bord Bia by specially trained Farm Liaison officers attached to each certified packing Center. Farms are audited at planned intervals, typically annually, by the Bord Bia inspector who also randomly carries out unannounced audits. This inspector is a highly trained person in quality systems, animal husbandry, veterinary aspects, record keeping and laboratory results.

There are several key aspects covered in the standard, including flock sourcing, hygiene, disease control, flock welfare, ongoing management on the site and environmental protection. The emphasis on hygiene and disease control is key to controlling salmonella. Under current Irish law, if a flock is found to be infected with salmonella, then the flock must be slaughtered out to protect the food supply chain, thus protecting the health of the consumer.

As an egg packer, our membership also depends on high levels of compliance at frequent audits. Accurate record keeping is required in the day-to-day operation as very intense scrutiny of product identification and traceability forms a huge part of Packing Centre audits. This ensures that if there is any breach of the quality chain the product can be traced back to the farm of origin and the cause can be identified right at the source.

The Standard is designed to offer the consumer peace of mind about the quality and safety of the egg. We are required to stamp the Bord Bia logo on each egg packed under the scheme and as a certified member we are forbidden from handling non Bord Bia eggs. I can say without a shadow of doubt that any egg carrying the Bord Bia Logo is an egg of the highest quality and poses no risk whatsoever to the consumer. This Bord Bia Sustainable Egg Assurance scheme is indeed proven to be "World Class."

Now I hope with that little package of information you will know how to choose your eggs and perhaps appreciate the effort made by the hen, the farmer and the packing center to provide you with food that is beyond reproach for quality, taste and safety.

The team at Margaret's 2019

CHAPTER FIVE

From Eggs to Helping Others

L ooking back on life most of it seems quite normal with a few standout highlights or even some lowlights. Throughout the good and bad times, our faith has served as a sustaining force that kept us going. That faith has also impacted our desire to give to others and be a blessing to them. One of the most memorable ways involves a television show and some determined producers, but it really allowed us to reach a larger audience than ever before.

A Humbling Opportunity

During the period in 2012 when we were moving toward the production of our pasteurized egg products, a busy time indeed, I was approached by a television show producer for the Secret Millionaire. They wanted to feature me on the show. I turned them down initially. I didn't have the time, we didn't have much available cash and I admit, I was a bit nervous about being on television. But it kept bothering me that I had said no. The premise of the show was to meet with charitable organisations and identify a handful that we could bring a little comfort or help of a financial nature to people less well off than ourselves. Was that not exactly what our hearts were longing to do? But, the idea of going on television was another story altogether.

Surprisingly enough, the producers got back in touch with me again the following year. They said that RTE had never made an episode themed on faith and that is what they were interested in doing if I agreed. That revelation made it very difficult to say no a second time. Having prayed about it, it seemed as if this was the direction that God wanted me to go and somehow the anxiety of being on the television faded. So, in July 2013 for 8 days, I lived in the heart of Dublin city, in an area known as the Liberties. Although it was different from my country lifestyle, I used to shop in the area when I lived in Dublin, so the area wasn't totally new to me. I expected to be humbled by the people I met, but nothing could have prepared me for the circumstances I encountered. Starting the journey, my emotions were ragged and mixed, I was happy to give back after receiving so much in our lives, I was a little nervous about my ability to pretend to be someone else for the purpose of the show. The biggest hurdle in my head was how I would have natural conversations with total strangers to find out as much as possible about them and their work without giving the game away. I need not have been concerned as from the moment I left home until my return I felt God, and my own Guardian Angel very close. The production team must also have been inspired as the week would eventually show.

Day one of filming started with a visit to St. Catherine's grotto. What an oasis of peace in the midst of the city's bustle and was it was so beautiful and so calming. Brother Bernard took care of the grotto and he was the one that took me to Carmen's Hall which was considered the heart of the Liberties. It was an old school that had been transformed into a community center. The place was busy from morning to night with so many activities from community center to a club, it offered so much to those living in the area. Here that I got to meet some of the individuals who are making a difference for their neighbors with hot meals, homework clubs and helpful advice. The community spirit that I encountered simply blew me away and made an indelible impression on the extended Farrelly family that has grown over the years.

The people I met were dealing with incredible circumstances. They had their feet firmly planted on the ground doing good for others day in and day out. That touched me. One man ran support groups for fathers whose kids were drug addicts. Through his own experiences, he identified a need for support, one that even the counselors hadn't seen. The members of the group acknowledged that counseling with their wives made it hard for them to open up. Imagine, your child dying of an overdose and the gardai arriving to your door with such news. These fathers found support within the group and their greater understanding of how each felt meant they could empathise and release their numerous emotions in a "sacred space," with other fathers in the same position. The group also organized events like drama, and they had a cycling club. These touched my heart because they trusted me completely and shared so much of their life's experience with me.

My encounters with the families with sick children made an everlasting impression on not only me but on family and staff members also. I left one house in a flood of tears after meeting a family with a three-year-old son who was almost halfway through treatment for leukemia. Their struggles were far reaching from the illness itself and related hospital stays and visits to dealing with a second baby on the way and daddy just recently started a new business. On top of all this, the washing machine broke down. Now bear in mind that the little boy is getting treatment, which while it hopefully is going well, it also makes some children very sick, so the washing mounts up. The demands were relentless and yet the overriding concern was with the little boy who needed a parent all of the time. This mammy told me about an event that sticks out in her mind: A family member was collecting some essentials to bring to the hospital and brought whatever the post had arrived. On opening the post, there was a cheque from Aoibheann's Pink Tie, a charity that helps with the practical needs of families on St John's Children's cancer ward in Crumlin Hospital. This cheque provided a new washing machine and helped with a mortgage payment. The instant relief was enormous and she and her family is forever grateful to the charity for making things a little less painful at that time. This family also demonstrated the strict cleaning routine for "Freddie" that takes place daily once the child is home. Freddie is what the children call the medical piece that is inserted in the chest to help with administering treatments and taking bloods. I also met with another family who was closer to the end of their cancer journey with their 7-year-old boy. On the day I called the young man was getting his redecorated bedroom back after Aoibheann's Pink Tie had done a mural on its wall.

The filming crew used the opportunity to capture the joy this act of kindness brought to the sick child and his family. This new charity, Aoibheann's Pink Tie, that I was hearing so much about was started by a man whose own daughter had died from cancer in 2010 at the age of 8 years old. I desperately wanted to meet this man, Jimmy Norman, and was completely overwhelmed by his story. During his family's time on St John's ward, he witnessed the great need that families were experiencing, especially those from the country. He pointed out that Aoibheann's Pink Tie charity could cover petrol, household bills, repairing washing or cooking equipment and sometimes just paying parking fees. They also had developed an overnight pack of practical bits and pieces as many families are referred from a country hospital and not only leave home empty handed but they are suddenly learning of a horrific diagnosis and bombarded with paperwork that needs signing without delay. All I can say now is that the whole team at Aoibheann's Pink Tie and the work they so generously do alerted me to something I took for granted, our children's health. What a shock to learn that 4 children are diagnosed each week with cancer. The children I met are some of the lucky ones as they had a good outcome but regrettably many do loose the battle just like that special little girl Aoibheann Norman and indeed my own sister who was still a child when diagnosed. I was still trying to digest it all when the program was aired. There followed a flood of emotion that I cannot quite describe but I do want to mention one mum who contacted me in appreciation. She watched the program in St John's ward at the bedside of her 5 months old daughter who at that time was undergoing treatment since being diagnosed a few days after her birth. The harrowing stories of these children, their resilience and that of the families is one of the most remarkable things I have ever experienced.

I couldn't help but realise that this was a bottomless pit of need. When I asked about his fundraising efforts, it was clear that even a big fundraiser couldn't address all the needs. It would just be a drop in the proverbial ocean. Yet, because he had firsthand experience, Jimmy was determined to keep chipping away at the mountain. It was amazing to me how he turned his own grief into something that so positively impacts others. Aoibheann's Pink Tie's mission made such an impression with me that we ended up partnering up with them beyond the making of the Secret Millionaire program.

Our white eggs come in a colorful pink box and a portion of the money goes to the charity. The distinctive box dresses up the very traditional egg stand and the white eggs with the mandatory pink ink jetting somehow just look like a great partnership to be proud of. In addition, these white eggs address demands from the diverse ethnic groups that have made Ireland their home.

It was particularly touching to me spending time with Jimmy, because I reflected on my own sister's fight with cancer. He brought me right back into the minds and hearts of my parents and how they must have felt with absolutely no support of any kind either practical or emotional. Her chances of survival were much slimmer back then, but the options for treatment have grown dramatically since. The emotional impact, however, on parents and families is still just as intense as it was then. There was a connection for me with these families and a deep sense of their struggles cut right deep into my heart.

The rest of my journey included visiting a choir that was inclusive for those with disabilities. The joy on the faces of the members was incredible. I loved watching them come together to make music and bring joy to their lives and those of others. The choir was led by a young lady who oozed passion for both the members and the music. While experiencing difficulties finding a permanent venue for their weekly sessions the choir continued to practice weekly and with the help of various services were able to but on concerts in some Dublin concert venues. Here I witnessed parents who would do simply anything they could to make their special children happy. Most of the members of the choir were adults, some were even homeless but the pride each had in their own individual talent was quite remarkable and their leader was another amazing person who impressed me that week.

The entire process made an everlasting impact on me, not as individuals, but for the causes and work they were involved in. The community center's team, feeding children and older community members, in the fashion of loaves and fishes, knew how to make a euro stretch and provide at least 2 balanced meals for the children. Parents who were struggling were had a firm, trusting supporting hand. Who wouldn't be moved by those people so willing to invest in their community? With much of the work done on a voluntary basis they are so deserving of total admiration. The lady in the community center told me that they got government support of €0.80 per child per day to give them two meals and provide the homework club. She also remarked that the traders working in the area like fruit & vegetable stores and butcher shops were very good to them.

Margaret helping with lunch at The Nicholas of Myra Centre in the heart of the Liberties, during filming of "The Secret Millionaire"

Liz from the Liberties Community & Margaret (immediately after announcing we were giving them a cheque)

My dear mother used say time and time again "If you have the heart to give, you will never want" and so it has been for us. Of course, life has not been easy, we have the normal ups and downs like everyone else but I guess it is our approach that makes us different. Our strong believe in God, our trust in His perfect timing and total acceptance that everything happens for a reason has brought many blessings on our family. Our trust in Him has been key to our decisions. Hard work pays off but with His blessing, success is much sweeter and more humbling.

In those few years following the appearance on the TV show, many doors opened to us helping to grow our business.

Lessons Learned

Along the way, we have learned some lessons that I want to share with others looking to dive into business for themselves. I also want to add that we are always learning, every day continues to be a school day in our lives. Being willing to ask questions and look to others for their expertise has helped us in many areas, including our growth into the pasteurized egg business. Here are just a few of the lessons we have learned.

Embrace Failure

Leo and I believe there's no such thing as failure, only feedback. When you try something new and it doesn't work out the way you planned, accept the lessons learned and use them to do it better the next time. Business success means that you will have failures too. It is a part of life that you must be willing to embrace. I guess that our trust in God and in our ability to make good decisions stems from our belief in approaching decisions, in faith rather than in fear. With an open mind, a willingness to accept feedback and a never give up attitude one can be more innovative and continue to be motivated by small successes.

Build on Basic Values

Our family's philosophy is not to take shortcuts, indeed there are few shortcuts available in business. The foundation on which most successful and sustainable businesses are built always includes a company culture that is built on basic traditional values of the owners. Our basic values are a willingness to work hard, be committed to our family, our business, our staff, our suppliers and our customers. Over the years, we have developed a reputation for being honest and honorable in our business dealings. The results have been a sustainable business for our family, but also one that we can look on with pride in the belief that many others both locally and further afield have benefited from our endeavors.

Focus on Your Uniqueness

Before anyone even starts a business, they need to identify their own Unique Selling Point or Value Proposition. Customers really need that product or service and you need to be able to provide it in a way that stands out from similar providers and of course it needs to be profitable for them. I have found that by sticking to our basic values, the quality of our product makes us stand out from our competition on multiple levels.

In recent years, we exhibited at shows like The Taste of Cavan, which is a regional food event hosting 120 stalls of artisan food and craft producers from Cavan and the surrounding areas and the 5 days Irish Gardening Festival, Bloom. We brought live hens to the event, creating a real farm to fork experience for the visitors. We partnered with a toy company, offering children the opportunity to play with ride on tractors and farm machinery and making our presence at the event a family experience. Our consumers got a chance to see where their eggs really come from and how the free-range process works. These events are exhausting, as one is on their feet and interacting with people all the time but the feedback, the thrill of face-to-face meeting with customers and joy on the faces of children and parents alike, enjoying the fun is where we get our rewards. Of course, we hope that the parents think of the Margaret's Brand when they shop for eggs in the future. Some parents have told us that because the children have such lovely memories of the event that they, the children insist on Margaret's Free Range Egg. This particularly makes me very happy as we are getting the message across to future shoppers ☺ ☺.

Taking part in this way makes us stand out from other free-range eggs producers. In reality our customer base has changed over the years. Immigration brought with it a demand for white eggs. The decision to separate whites from yolks at the beginning of the pasteurising process was a really good one as it gave us many more options. When developing this product range, we were not fully aware of all the eventual uses for our products. When our egg whites in 500gm and 1000gm bottles arrived on the market, they were in huge demand by people who wanted to build muscle and limit their fat intake. We were now meeting a new need for our consumers, and this is one of the reasons why I say that our decisions were somehow guided. Standing out from our competition indeed!

Reawakening My Faith

In Jan 2003 I was contacted late one night by my friend. We had not met for years but have the type of friendship that is very relaxed and can be switched on exactly where we left off last time. Kay words were, "Maggie, would you come to Medjugorje in May. I'm contacting Catherine and a few others also. You don't have to answer me now, but I will call you back during the week." It was 23.45 and I was awakened out of my sleep, so I muttered okay and went right back to sleep.

A few evenings later when I returned home from a church meeting Leo said, "Your friend Kay called to check if you were going." My reaction was that I'd completely forgotten about her call, but Leo's answer shocked me. "I told her you would go," he said.

Our group of about 60 pilgrims from Ireland, organised by Joe Walsh Tours, arrived in Medjugorje on the evening of Sunday May 4th to the sound of heavenly music filling the air. I knew nothing about the place really but was relieved at the thought of getting a whole week's break from the everyday activities at home and relished the thoughts of catching up with my friends Kay and Catherine and Catherine's sister Teresa. I did recall mammy once telling me that she heard on the radio that children in a country in eastern Europe were seeing Our Lady every evening and Mammy was overjoyed to learn that the sun was dancing in the sky. Also, a family friend Rose, my late sister's godmother, had a daughter Kathy, who being generous with her time and her life had volunteered in a place where war was raging. The place sounded like Medjugorje. Unknown to me Kathy had married a local man and was actually settled there. My first impression was one of awe at the crowds, the devotion of the locals and pilgrims alike and the how very simple the place was, compared with other more commercialised sites visited by the mother of God.

After Mass on day one, we got an introduction to the week ahead by Philip Ryan the JWT representative in Medjugorje and met our guide for the week. Philip's story and how he came to be there impressed me. Like a lamb I followed the group's itinerary, attending Holy Mass in English at 10am daily in the church of St James. The church could no longer accommodate all the pilgrims, so the ceremonies were transmitted via speakers to the outdoors. The weather was glorious, even at 10am the sun was so strong, it was important for me to find shade. As a group, we climbed Apparition Hill and Cross Mountain. We prayed at the Blue Cross, the site of Our Lady's first Apparition. We attended the evening ceremonies without understanding a word as they were held in Croatian but yet there was something compelling us to attend. As we climbed Apparition Hill, I noticed one pilgrim being helped by 3 others. Just for a moment imagine a steep rocky mountainside crowded with people climbing at the same time. I later discovered that the man being helped was in fact totally blind. He had such a desire to get to the top of the site of Apparitions that the generosity just switched on in the hearts of others and they helped make his desire become a reality. That was first of many lessons of gratitude. As days one and two passed, a sense of calmness and peace surrounded me that I could not have believed existed. There was so much to see, so much to experience and so little time to fit all in that I began to wonder why I thought this week might be a holiday from my busy life in Mullagh.

In the evenings long queues formed outside of St James Church for Confessions. There were dozens of priests available, some in the confessionals and many sitting on chairs in the open air. One evening mid-week, nervously I joined a queue. It had been a long time and I wasn't quite sure what to expect. Secretly, I hoped the priest would not fully understand my mumblings. I entered the confessional where a lovely young priest from the Czech Republic greeted me with a welcoming handshake. He told me a little about himself and asked many questions about me. We seemed to be chatting for quite some time and I was beginning to wonder when I should begin to off load my pre-prepared list of indiscretions.

Suddenly like a great flash of lightening I realised this young man is helping me examine my conscience and instantly too I felt that somehow, he knew what my answers should be. To my great relief, we had already travelled through almost all the 10 Commandments. The outpouring of God's Mercy and with such an overwhelming abundance of His Grace I accepted the absolution given me in the priests blessing and he finished by asking me to evangelise on my return home to Ireland. I was in tears leaving the confessional. How naive and stupid I'd been forgetting the power of God and how "His power working through us can do infinitely more than we can either ask or imagine" (Ephesian's 3:20). My tears were tears of relief, tears of joy and tears of humility. I honestly did not know what evangelise meant but I knew for sure why Medjugorje has come to be known as "The Confessional of the world"! My life changed forever in those few minutes. I thank God for that wonderful priest and for the gifts of Trust and Patience bestowed on me in that encounter. Since that first pilgrimage to Medjugorje I cannot worry. That indeed is quite a miracle as prior to 2003 there seemed to be always things to worry about.

Early on the morning of May 11th, as our group prepared to return home, I accidently turned on my ankle causing an injury. During the bus ride to Dubrovnik and the flight to Dublin the pain was excruciating. A doctor who was on our pilgrimage suggested to have an x-ray once we got to Dublin. As the journey from Dublin airport took us through Navan I decided to go to the hospital there. Our parish priest who happened to be at the hospital visiting when we stopped at A&E laughed at me saying "A ha, you run to Medjugorje looking for miracles and you break your foot, good enough for you." He was joking of course, and I replied, "And you know what Father, I'll be going again." I knew I would go again but did not know when or how.

Late in the 2004, the small group of friends joined another pilgrimage group to Medjugorje. There was no time to waste. I wanted to make the most of every minute and could not wait for the opportunity to get to confessions. Without having a second Road to Damascus experience this time, I longed for Leo to make it to Medjugorje and wished him to experience the love of God as I did. This time we were more engaged with the spirit of the pilgrimage from day one and I felt called to become a group leader. I made the necessary enquiries and even followed up on our return home but being a little prone to procrastination I made no decision.

Early in 2005, I had occasion to speak with Rose and during the conversation she asked if we were going to Medjugorje. I'd been hesitant, and had done nothing to make it happen but she said, "Now that Aerlingus are flying to Dubrovnik from Easter, why don't you just go it alone and Kathy will send transport for you. She and Luka have their building to a certain stage now and can keep guests." I think that was the nudge I needed: Leo decided to come, we got a priest who was willing to accompany us and along with Kay, Catherine, Teresa and 2 others we experienced another grace filled pilgrimage. While I did not at the time consider this to be a group, as such, it actually turned out to be the beginning of yet another journey in my life and since then, I have organised, with Kathy's help, 2 group pilgrimages annually.

Last year, of course, COVID-19 demanded we stay put. The group size varied from 30 to 65 pilgrims and over the years we have witnessed many miracles in people's lives. I'm not sure, if even now I know the true meaning of evangelise but I know for sure that for every pilgrimage organised, every pilgrim we help and for every prayer we say we are blessed a hundredfold. I can no longer worry about anything, considering worry to be a great waste of energy. I truly believe that, in all matters, God's timing is perfect, and He has also blessed me with the patience to wait on His timing. This blessing however can be a problem when others, who do not understand, see my treasured gift as a lack of motivation. In this, I see a great example of God's wonderful sense of humor.

CHAPTER SIX

Changes for Our Eggs

Well now that we have reached this point in the story, I am thinking what more is there to say. I am now a 3-time granny with all the joys that goes with that status, not forgetting the creaking, stiffening joints. I have swollen feet, sore joints, and medication for almost every ailment – I jest. Life has been just wonderful, and I regularly ask myself where those years went. I watch our grandchildren and my heart bursts with excitement for them and their parents. Having these little children growing up beside us is such a privilege and fills every day with magic.

Back at the beginning 2020, we could not have imagined what was lurking just around the corner and maybe we are not even close to the end. We seem to be entering a whole new era but I'm sure that there are plenty more surprises ahead. Over the past few months, both Leo and I have been cocooning for the most part on account of the COVID-19 pandemic. "You are not yet the age to require that action," I hear you say. Yes, but with my asthma I feel more comfortable not to be in public as I spend a lot of time coughing. Our little granddaughter, Lucy, was born right at the beginning of the "lockdown" and so we had to wait 10 long weeks before being able to see her properly or hold her.

Jack, our 4-year-old grandson, would say when he would see Leo or I, "Mammy are the germs gone yet?" Tadgh who was just beginning to string words together, actually began making sentences during that time. Jack who goes to primary school in September experienced great excitement just yesterday when he attended playschool through a Zoom call for the first time. His mam Aileen used her mobile phone which gave me a little chuckle as I thought back to my early days in the bank and the introduction of computerization. The computer filled a whole floor on quite a substantial building. How things have changed! Makes me wonder what the next 50 years will bring.

One day at lunch as we discussed some recent events and how political correctness has become such an influencing factor in our lives, someone said, "Margaret, in your life you have witnessed some amount of change."

"Yes," I replied, "but what are you referring to?" Then the answer came.

"The other day you said that when you were a child Catholics would be excommunicated if they entered a Protestant Church and only recently the Archbishop of Dublin Dr Martin attended the Muslim event in Croke Park." The person was shocked that anyone might even care about religious beliefs. Yes, I agreed that was a change of seismic proportions! I'm not suggesting he was right or wrong but that just summed up a level of change in one aspect of life, in my lifetime that could not have been foreseen back in those days. We have just come through a period when our Holy Mass could not be celebrated in public because of the coronavirus. Indeed, this has been a challenging time. I could not have envisaged the likes and sometimes wonder what our parents might make of it all.

From the latter weeks of 2019, Ireland has experience unprecedented challenges in her poultry industry. About 25% of the country's laying hens had to be slaughtered as a result of Avian Influenza putting enormous pressure on the supply chain for eggs at retail. With COVID-19 restrictions, food service was out of action so we were able to redirect eggs through our grading system that were originally produced for the breaking and pasteurising. As our production to meet demand depends on a constant rolling of restocking with new flocks into our overall flock we continue to hope and pray that we can avoid the Avian Influenza challenge. It is necessary to practice heightened bio-security at times like this to ensure that all possible known vectors for the disease are controlled in so far as possible.

So far, we have been impacted only in an operational sense as thank God our staff have remained free of the coronavirus and all hens supplying us have escaped the Avian Influenza virus. This was the year where we had planned great things. Our Margaret's brand has been in stores for a year or so and we planned much promotional activity to increase awareness and hopefully sales. Trusting in God's perfect timing and that all things happen for a reason; we accept that the right time for the Margaret's Road Show was not to be 2020.

Has business taught me any lessons? The answer is a resounding yes. In business, every day is a "school day" and anyone who thinks otherwise is far mistaken. One must stay positive to succeed. Each day will sling new challenges in your direction but if you are a "can do" person well then you will find the perfect solution and get on with it. If you later discover that the solution was just about less than perfect you will revise, restructure, and reengage and before long the light at the end of the tunnel will get brighter. Many years ago, I found a poster which said, "Is that a light at the end of the tunnel or could it just be another so & so bringing me more work." At the time life felt very much like the latter but a positive attitude overcomes all that and I have always believed in Henry Ford's moto, "Whether you believe you can or you can't, you are right."

Would I do anything differently? I think I would do nothing terribly different. When we were growing up and were not well off financially mammy regularly reminded us that "it is no sin to be poor, it is just awkward," and having given us a strong work ethic we knew that once we were prepared to apply ourselves to a job and work to make things happen, the rewards would come. We can in fact learn more from mistakes or setbacks than we learn from constant success and so each hiccup or challenge was viewed as an opportunity to learn: next time do it differently and have a better outcome. Having a young family and managing the business was filled with challenges needing constant prioritising. While I put business before family on many occasions simply because the customer was our livelihood, I do not really regret that decision. The children for the most part have a good work ethic as a result and they do realise that everything including success comes at a cost.

Any regrets? Life with all its ups and downs has been good for the most part so what is there to regret.

Advise to someone starting out in business? Leave more financial value on one's own time. It's is very tempting to undervalue one's own time in an attempt to be more competitive but if the day comes when you need to pay someone to do what you once did but undervalued, it is really difficult to get the price of the product up sufficiently to remain sustainable.

Highlights and amazing memories? Some memories are imprinted on my memory but not because they are good ones. I sometimes get very angry when I see very well-intended animal rights people advocate for protection of foxes. I have 2 lasting memories of interaction between the foxes and our beloved hens. On one occasion a parent fox decided that our paddock was an ideal training ground for her cubs and in the space of 10 minutes they had slaughtered about 40 beautiful hens. The young do not kill clean, so the poor hens were mauled and some just beheaded and left lying there. Lest anyone should think that we do not protect the hens there is a fence around the perimeter of the paddocks that is almost 2 meters high. On examining the fencing after this event, we discovered that the parent fox climbed over the fence, even though there is an electric wire running around the outside about 0.3m from the ground. Once she gained access, then she scratched away the clay from under the fence and the little ones could gain access without touching the electrified fencing. I'm sure you have heard "cute as an old fox." Well, this is firsthand evidence how true that saying is because she scratched the ground on the inside so she could avoid shocks from the electric fence.

Another occasion back in the very early days, when our accommodations were not purpose build, but farm buildings suitably adapted to accommodate the hens, stands out also. The floor level of the hen house was about 1.5 meters above the level of the ground outside, so we made a platform at floor level and built pallets to enable the hens to safely come down to the outdoor paddock level. It was fun watching them pop up and down the structure where they could effortlessly move to and from the house. One morning while I was still in the hen house after opening the door to the outside, I heard a pitiful cry from outside. As I approached the spot where the crying was, I discovered a hen disappearing underneath the ramp. When Leo investigated, he discovered that a fox had made her den underneath the foundation of the henhouse and a family of cubs now lived with her there. That cute lady was not travelling far for meals.

In business the good memories are far too numerous to mention but I think winning the European award for women in farming was the highlight. Leo, Anne Marie, and I travelled to Brussels where we were given a royal welcome by the Irish Farmers Association there. This happened because a year earlier I had been selected as Irish Farm Woman of the year at the Women and Agriculture Annual Conference.

In Brussels we were treated like we were very important folks and our host for the duration was a wonderful lady Maura Dillon who has become a friend for life. I must admit that we, well perhaps I should say, I felt like a "fish out of water" but what an experience. On that occasion too, we met Irish MEP's, Marian Harkin, Mairead McGuinness, Phil Hogan and Sean Kelly, all who gave time to join us for the occasion of the ceremony. I have met Mairead McGuinness on a number of occasions since and she stills remember our names. What a woman and what a great representative for Ireland.

Copa-Cogeca award Ceremony in Brussels L-R Maura Dillon, IFA, Leo Margaret, AnneMarie, Mairead McGuinness (EU Commissioner) & Liam McHale (IFA Director in Brussels) 2016

*Outside Parliament buildings Brussels Maura Dillon (IFA) Mairead
Lavery (Irish Farmers journal) Margaret & Liam McHale*

Any unfulfilled dream? I achieved most things that I aimed to achieve, in
fact my achievements were far greater than my expectations reminding,
me that God in His generosity actually does do infinitely more that we
can either ask or imagine. Less successful or failed ventures do not
weigh heavy on me in the belief that each outcome probably was for

the best. What I would wish for now is that Leo & I could relax a little while the company continues to grow. For now, I would like to stay a little connected to the business and will be completely happy when every decision does not depend on my input. It is wonderful to feel so appreciated and indeed needed but none of us are indispensable and so I would be happy to watch from the side lines as the company flourishes. With new challenges like these viruses causing self-isolation, lockdowns, supply chain shortages and heightened bio-security to mention but a few I call on my faith to try to understand what the purpose of it all is and I have come to the conclusion that even in this fast-developing age of science and IT, man still does not have full control. I am so glad that God came back into my life in 2003 and am so thankful for His love and Mercy. I cannot fear for the future no matter what is ahead.

From the very start we could not spend huge amounts of money, so we made best use of the available resources in terms of facilities, space, equipment, people, and financial funds. We still operate from our own yard where the accommodation was adapted to facilitate the needs at the time. There has been a number of upgrades over the years and while we are not a modern plant like some of our competition, the customers for Margaret's products will not find an egg in the whole wide world that compares with our eggs for flavor & passion. You can indeed "Taste the Difference!"

CHAPTER SEVEN

In The End, A New Beginning

Just like building the business, the story of our family's journey has taken years to complete and I often found myself wondering if I would ever get there! The truth is this story is not mine alone but involves 2 sets of parents, siblings, my dear beloved Leo, our children and now grandchildren. It's also important to remember that very many people outside of the family contributed much more to the success of the family business than I can quantify in these chapters.

Despite the various challenges, as we look back those difficulties really were personal growth opportunities. No-one was more surprised than Leo & I at how the company grew from a micro business to a thriving enterprise that one day would belong to the next generation. That thought never crossed our minds in those early days, and I do believe that if it had occurred to us were would most likely have been scared of the future. As I ask myself the question: What was the key"? The overwhelming thought invades my mind and I realise that our motivation to "never let anyone down" overruled all else and once a commitment was made expectations were met no matter what the cost in time and effort! Selling the eggs of 150 birds in those early days was the challenge of that day but moving times and bigger stocking numbers presented new challenges and greater leaps of faith.

Everything in life is about right timing! Try to rush something and the results can be disappointing, yet we were feeling the obvious pressures of an aging couple. Having, many years ago, appointed God as our CEO, placing everything to His hands, and trusting His Wisdom and Vision, we knew that the company's future path would one day be clear, in His time and in His unique Way. Patience, we have learned, is key to getting the best out of everything in life.

While our children all worked in the business, allowing us to tap into their various talents, no one stood out as the natural, apparent successor, one who would take over and be groomed to lead the team. Their talents and strengths gelled around the leadership Leo and I created.

Still, we faced the challenges that all businesses do as they grow. It's been increasingly difficult to find individuals who are willing to or who could give the level of commitment needed. Behind the scenes of a thriving egg business there is a lot of hard work. On the farm, hens need to be cared for and eggs need to be collected whether you are sick or want to sleep in. They don't keep to a calendar, so there are no days off for public holidays or religious observances. At the packing center the demands are endless. Customers expect their "Egg fixture" to be kept replenished and excuses are not entertained. The modern-day shopper is always under time pressure and so are not interested in spending time in the egg category. A well-presented space with eye catching packaging is a huge help. In this very aspect we had set ourselves a very high standard for which we have no regrets. Satisfied customers to us meant a "job well done". The outstanding challenge during the pandemic has been availability of committed staff. We did have stand out talent on our team but today's business world makes huge demands on management teams. Our team while experienced and very capable, depended more and more on Roberto who we identified as the one person who could possibly manage the company in the future.

We must have been doing something right in the eyes of others as from time to time, competitors showed interest in our company, but such a dramatic change never felt quite right. Months of lockdown, Covid restrictions, continued uncertainties, social distancing, vaccination do's and don'ts, virtual meetings, and our Churches closed to public worship, all presented unprecedented challenges. This coupled with mounting industry struggles imposing their own set of pressures led to renewed evaluation of our position. What an incredible experience the last 18 months have been!

While plotting and praying about our business' next move, we got an expression of interest from a competitor. What surprised us was their total acknowledgement of our hard work, the recognition of our particular interest in establishing a "Brand with personality" and their total respect for our ethos. There were many lengthy discussions on how, selling the business might impact our family, those who worked for us, the families of our suppliers and anyone else who in one way or another depended on us for their individual livelihoods.

Yet, as a wife and mother, I also saw the potential blessings. From time to time the children had expressed an interest in different pursuits and this would allow them to do that. Further investment in upgrading equipment and premises would be required in the next few years to keep up standards and to remain sustainable. The thoughts of taking on huge debt, and leaving that as our legacy to those who had helped us achieve so much was a huge consideration as we are still a small company with limited economies of scale. Furthermore, it seemed very clear to us that the future lay in added value products and we were ideally positioned to take advantage of that possibility given how our pasteurizing plant operated. Although willing to start new projects that would enable the business to grow, I was beginning to feel my body say "slow down, you cannot keep up this pace forever" I was ready for a break, and so was Leo. It was always our vision to leave something wonderful for the next generation. As with many family businesses, there are challenges with transitioning to the next generation. Maintaining ownership could mean Roberto, who was serving as our managing director, would be taking on the business and managing it on his own. In an industry that worldwide is battling with many challenges and needing to find endless solutions to sustainability and welfare pressures we feared that our "treasured 5th child" could become somewhat of a poisoned chalice for its next management team.

I can truly say that if any of our children had been really invested in taking the reins and running the business full-time, we likely would not be considering any offers. While they all have worked hard to grow the business, everyone had their unique role with no one showing forth as the natural successor or demonstrated a willingness to take it on. Hence, Leo and I felt confident that being open to this offer was wise for our family. Our long-term dreams and those of others could well be realized as part of a bigger team. New ownership, new leadership and greater resources could provide a future that would be less difficult and more prepared to deal with the challenges of lasting sustainability.

The end of this chapter is in sight both from the point of view of the book itself and the business. Clonarn Clover and Margaret's now have new owners but Leo and I will continue to keep hens and produce free range eggs. Our pasteurizing facility transferred as a going concern, while our egg grading facility is redundant with all the eggs now being processed in a beautiful recently refurbished, state of the art premises less than an hour away. Members of our staff, particularly my right-hand man Roberto, have transitioned with the company to the new owners. While we are upheaving his life, I believe there is huge opportunity for his personal growth within the new, bigger and better resourced company. The new owners are eager to work with him and he knows the business inside and out. I am confident that Roberto who has been a huge asset to us will also prove to be an asset to the new owners as he brings with him a valuable wealth of experience in innovation and New Product Development.

With regards to our three children who have worked most of their working life with us, their position is a little less certain as the individual roles covered by two of them in our company are already filled in the other company. This I find sad and watching how they each view their position currently is quite painful but here is where trust in God's plan helps also.

Endings can be sad, but beginnings are exciting. Right now, we have a mix of both. Leo and I have put so much into our hens and growing this business that letting go was not easy. Yet, everything happens in God's timing, and it is clear that this is the right time for this transition to the next season of our lives. Deep in my heart I believe we are doing the right thing even though for some people change may be difficult but will offer surprising new personal development opportunities. For Leo & I, retirement will feel strange but I know too that God has a plan and my only wish and desire is to do God's will. I guess as we get older these thoughts become more of a priority!

I hope that you have enjoyed learning about our business and our family. That you have learned a little of what happens to bring fresh eggs to the supermarket or shop where you buy your groceries. I would like too that you have gained a small appreciation for those little hens who are marvelous creatures of nature and work so hard to please us all. We are both grateful at having decided to go into this business as the blessings it has brought our family over the years are innumerable. During the most challenging times of our lives the hens demanded consistency in their routines and this "must do" served as a great grounder and motivator to keep going.

For Leo & I the memories are rich, indeed each of the children too have reminisced with smiles on past years and events.

Here is where I say "thank you" for coming on our journey with me and for being present as we say good-bye to day to day managing the business we loved dearly. Every ending is the beginning of something new and it is with the greatest of joy that we look to the future and fingers crossed watch our treasured baby grow and mature in the hands of someone else, while Leo & I return to the beginning and concentrate on producing eggs and looking after our dearly loved hens.

The Farrelly family on a night out in 2015
(Leo, Killian, Aileen, AnneMarie, Edel & Margaret)

Author the Author

Margaret Farrelly is an author, business owner and free-range expert. Her family business began as an additional income stream before becoming the family's main source of revenue. For over thirty years her husband Leo and their children have contributed to the growth of their egg business. Margaret's is the largest independent supplier of free-range eggs in Ireland.

As the children grew older, she returned to education through government supported schemes and focused her learnings on business, agri-food and where possible poultry. Applying the new learnings led to the company becoming an industry leader in innovation and animal welfare. This in turn lead to Margaret winning awards like: Gold Medal at Taste of Cavan Awards (2013) and Cavan Food and Drink Most Innovative Business Award (2013) and Cavan Business Person of the Year (2013) also. Two years later awards came flowing again with Provincial Winner of the Ulster Bank Business Achievers Food and Drink Award (2015); The Love Irish Food, Masters of Their Art Award (2015); Ms. Farrelly also won the FBD Women & Agriculture Award for On Farm Innovation (2016). The highlight of awards came when the Irish Farmers Association /The Irish Farmers Journal entered Margaret in Europe's Innovation Award for Women Farmers 2017; a Pan European competition developed by **Copa**-Cogeca.

She achieved a Diploma in Applied Poultry Science at The University of Scotland in Ayr in 2012 and in 2019 with the support of Cavan Local Enterprise Office, became a Tangent student at Trinity College for a Post Graduate Certificate in Innovation & Entrepreneurship Development.

Having spent 12 years in the banking industry prior to returning to the country and getting involved in farming, Ms Farrelly believes, even the wildest dream is achievable with the right attitude, but most likely will require a lot of hard work and unwavering determination.

Ms. Farrelly's upbringing instilled in her a fondness for caring and sharing. She admits she is very lucky that the love of her life and partner in all walks of life mirrors these characteristics. Together they get pleasure in giving and have helped a number of charities both local and national over the years. Additionally, Ms. Farrelly is a devout Catholic, who regularly visits Our Lady's Shrine at Knock in Co Mayo. She has made a number of pilgrimages to Lourdes and has been to Medjugorje on at least 30 occasions.

She is married with 4 children, three of which are involved in the family business. The oldest is living and working in Australia.